What I Love About Cricket

Sandy Balfour

EBURY
PRESS

3 5 7 9 10 8 6 4 2

Published in 2009 by Ebury Press, an imprint of Ebury Publishing
A Random House Group Company

The Random House Group Limited Reg. No. 954009

Addresses for companies within the Random House Group can be found at www.randomhouse.co.uk

A CIP catalogue record for this book is available from the British Library

The Random House Group Limited supports The Forest Stewardship Council (FSC), the leading international forest certification organisation. All our titles that are printed on Greenpeace approved FSC certified paper carry the FSC logo. Our paper procurement policy can be found at www.rbooks.co.uk/environment

FSC
Mixed Sources
Product group from well-managed forests and other controlled sources
www.fsc.org Cert no. TT-COC-2139
© 1996 Forest Stewardship Council

Printed in the UK by CPI Mackays, Chatham, ME5 8TD

ISBN 9780091927318

What I Love About Cricket

This is a romance. At least half of it is true.

Contents

PROLOGUE

The companionship of the long-distance run chase

It's the most basic cricket equation. One hundred and forty-six runs to win with 40 overs and ten wickets in hand. That's three and a half and a bit per over. Easy. And it's a perfect day for it. The pitch is a little soft and the grass a little long, but who cares? The sun is shining, the cows across the hedgerow are lowing and all is well with the world. We're playing on a field on the far northern edge of London. I think it's Hertfordshire, but I could be wrong. London's county fringe always confuses me. When do the 32 boroughs become Essex? The field is one of those you find dotted between the northern fringe of London and the M25. In the war it would have been an airfield. You can imagine the hangars, a few Spitfires, a wooden hut with a telephone. A siren on a pole. The pilots on standby. It would have been a day like today. A few light clouds in the pale blue sky. A gentle breeze tickling the leaves of the oak, chestnut and hawthorn trees that surround the field. Sorry, landing strip. The chaps – fighter pilots were always 'chaps', weren't they? – sit on wooden chairs and read the papers or play cards. They swap cigarettes and write letters. From time to time they scan the sky to the east and pretend not to care. Nowadays we can hear occasional traffic, but back then it is quiet, too quiet. And then the telephone rings...

Our changing room looks as if it hasn't been touched since 1940. Once leather flight jackets would have hung on the cast-iron hooks that line one peeling wall. The door creaks wearily on rusted hinges. Where the pilots once ran, grabbing their kit before reaching for the skies... now it's our opening batsmen. They strap on their pads and tuck their boxes into their jockstraps. Some of them have helmets. They grab bats and gloves, inners and thigh pads. We pat them on the back.

'Have a look,' says the skipper, meaning 'Don't do anything stupid'.

'Good luck,' we say. I'm standing with the skipper, a tall, gangling football fanatic called Rob. We watch the openers take guard. We look up at the sun. We check our watches.

'Should be alright,' says Rob. Rob hates losing almost as much as he hates Tories, which is a lot.

'Not many teams can match our attack,' I say.

This is true, at least in the league in which we play. Our attack consists largely of a 40-something man we call The Undertaker. The Undertaker can land his military medium pacers on a penny and that's what he does, for over after over. They land just short of a length and just outside off stump. Sometimes they cut in. Sometimes they hit the seam and move away. They're never very fast and they slow down the longer he bowls. It drives batsmen to distraction. The Undertaker's bowling looks as if it should be easy to hit, but somehow it isn't and so batsmen play stupid shots and get out. As an attacking formula it works a treat. Which is why we're chasing only 146 to win.

'I see no problem,' I say as the problems begin. Ells edges his first ball to the slips and, in a flagrant flouting of all we hold dear, the fat guy in the Hush Puppies catches the thing and – to add insult to injury – makes it look easy. He holds the ball to his belly the way you sometimes see a drunk cradling a pint. Next up is Ben. Ben is one of the colts just making the transition into the senior teams. One day he's going to be very good. He has movie-star looks and a text-book technique. Unfortunately there are no cameras and we don't play on text-book grounds. He strides forward to his first ball, but it is held up a little by the pitch. It pops off his bat and is neatly pocketed by the bowler. Two down… One hundred and forty-six to win. Simple maths, really.

'Jesus,' says Rob. He has put me at number eight and himself at seven. He didn't think we'd be needed. Now suddenly…

'Christ,' he says.

The fielding side are enjoying this. Third ball of the innings and their bowler is on a hat-trick. You can hear them chirping and whooping. The skipper signals the field to come in. He's got six catchers within ten yards of the bat. Plus the keeper and the bowler. The other three fielders are positioned for mis-hit slogs. One at mid-wicket, one at cover point and one somewhere between third man and fly slip. Not that anyone in our team would be that stupid. When the opposition bowler is on a hat-trick, what you do is block the next ball. Even if it's a slow full toss. You block it, the fielders all clear off to the boundary whence they came, and the game goes on. Everyone knows that.

Except for Nick. Every club has a guy like Nick. Mind you, every club has a guy like Rob. Nick has a fine resonant frame, a cheerful smile and a penchant for the slog sweep. He arrives half awake and plays half asleep. His socks don't match and his trousers don't fit. But he can hit that ball. Nick's eye is so good he sometimes forgets to take guard. One time he forgot his bat. But not today. Today he is fully equipped (pads, box, bat, gloves, helmet, fags) and properly briefed. No room for misinterpretation. None of this 'have a look' nonsense. Nick and Rob have known each other a long time. The skipper cuts right to the chase: 'Don't do anything fucking stupid,' he says. 'Don't get out. Don't try to hit the skin off good balls. Don't…'

Nick's first ball is neither good nor bad. It doesn't have time to be. It's barely left the bowler's hand before Nick is charging down the pitch. I don't know. Maybe he's remembered he only drank half his pint and wants to get back before some other bugger finishes it. Or maybe he thinks there's a war on. Maybe he sees German fighter planes coming over the hill. This is death-wish cricket. In the Great War he would have been first over the top. Nick meets the ball halfway down the pitch, slightly in front of the guy fielding at silly mid-wicket. He opens his shoulders, turns his body and takes aim at the phantom Messerschmitt he's spotted over square leg. Only he doesn't quite catch it right. He's through the shot too early and the ball flies off the top edge of his bat towards the sun.

'Mine!' shouts the bloke who has come in from third man for just such a shot.

He too makes the catch look easy. Our opponents swamp their bowler in a delighted heap.

'Our Lady of Infinite Mercy,' says Rob. So early in the innings and already he's running out of deities. He watches Nick make the long, slow walk of shame back to the Pavilion. Nothing on *The Weakest Link* can compare with what a batsman endures as he leaves the field after getting out to a shot he should never have played. Not with the score the way it is.

Which at the moment is nought for three. Or, as the Aussies would say, three for nought.

'Mother of Buddha,' says Rob, which throws me for a moment. Did Buddha have a mother? They never taught us that in catechism.

We survive the rest of the over unscathed. And the one after that. But something happens to a team when they lose early wickets. Think of those cartoon lemmings following each other over the sea cliff. An LBW here, a clean bowled there, a silly run out for good measure and we're 32 for six off ten overs when I join Rob at the crease. The sun is still shining. The magnificent oaks still stir in the breeze. The cows continue to chew their thoughtful cud. But the day is unaccountably darker and more gloomy.

And we're 114 runs short of our target.

We pretend to back up. When Rob's batting I walk a little way down the pitch in case he calls me for a quick one. He does the same for me. But we both know it's a con. We're only going to run the slowest of slow singles. For a few overs anyway. We're going to 'have a look', like grown-ups. We're going to get our eyes in. And then we're going to win. Also like grown-ups. At the end of the first over we meet in the middle and punch gloves, like comic-book professionals. I am Frasier to his Niles. He is all nervous energy and swooning enthusiasm. I am effortlessly superior incompetence. He pats down an imaginary fault in the pitch the way Niles cleans his seat in that coffee shop in Seattle.

'Doing anything after?' Rob asks. He's only being polite. He knows I have children and therefore, in his eyes, have no life. I shrug.

'Some people are coming over.'

'The boy wonder?'

'Him too.'

Rob chuckles. I've told him before that my daughter has a boyfriend. And that said boyfriend doesn't play cricket.

'You'd better make some runs then. Give yourself something to boast about.'

'I can always lie.'

'Again?'

We block out another over. The opposing team have sensed our nervousness. They bring on a leg spinner who bowls with uncanny accuracy and prodigious amounts of turn. I have to watch every ball like a hawk. We each score a single and meet again in the middle.

'You?'

'There's someone.'

'A date?'

Rob looks at the pitch. I look at the sky.

'Keep going,' he says and battle resumes.

We manage not to get out for three overs. It's very hot. The pitch is hardening up a little. The opposition are wilting. The bowling becomes more ragged. In his third over the leg spinner lobs up a full toss on leg stump. It's only polite to hit it into the fields beyond the trees. A straight drive (well, straightish; no one in my club will believe it if I say I hit a *straight* drive) for four and things are looking up. The 50 comes and goes and with it the drinks break. Often the drinks break will bring a wicket. The fielders feel rejuvenated and the batsmen lose their concentration. But we manage to survive it.

Between overs Rob and I pump gloves.

'Anyone nice?' I ask.

He shrugs.

It's a funny business, falling in love. My girlfriend and I did it so long ago we sometimes forget. And now my children? Earlier in the year my daughter fell for a boy. When I told Rob about it, he laughed.

'Just be glad,' he said. 'Women can't date men who play cricket.'

Why?

Well, the time for one thing. Saturday nights become unpredictable. 'I'll see you when the game ends,' is not much of a promise when the game can end anywhere between 5 and 9 pm. Focus, for another. People on dates like your undivided attention. During the cricket season my attention is always divided. Dennis Nordern made his gentle joke about it. 'A funny month, October,' he mused. 'It's when the true cricket fan realises his wife left him in May.'

Their new young bowler pops one up outside off stump. I slash it straight to point. He drops it and Rob calls me through for a single. Now we're in the ascendancy. Ten overs left, 50 to get and they're dropping their catches. The fielders have stopped chirping at us. There's always a couple in every team, the ones who make a noise and yell at their teammates between balls. But the rest of the team have fallen silent. They just want to get this over with. One of them, a young guy with floppy hair, looks a lot like my daughter's boyfriend. At least I think he does. You can't really see his face. But he has the same kind of body. Sort of long and gangly. Like he's done all his growing, and the body weight is only now catching up. Same sort of shyness. When his skipper tells him to move he does it without comment. When his hair hangs down in front of him it's hard to tell what – or even if – he's thinking. With Rob on strike I have time to watch him. Now that I look at him, he is the spitting image of the boy wonder. Something about the way he holds himself. The way he keeps his athleticism in reserve. And he's coming on to bowl.

A change of bowler always creates a moment of interest. In Test cricket you know what to expect. Bowlers don't surprise you. They may bowl badly or well, but essentially they do what they did the week before. At our level, though, you don't know what you're getting until the first ball is bowled. Will it be some hopeless kid who's only there because they were short of numbers, or some guy who's made the London Schools side for the past three years and whose uncle used to play for Worcestershire? Only the first ball will tell.

Rob and I meet in the middle of the pitch.

'Have a look,' he says. The kid is bowling a few practice balls to a teammate. He has a nice action, straight, high arm, looking over his left shoulder.

'Change of bowler,' says the umpire. 'Right arm over.'

For form's sake I take guard again. Make it look like I know what I'm doing. The kid is waiting to bowl. He fiddles with something on a chain round his neck and then tucks it inside his shirt. It's a gesture I've seen a lot in recent weeks. The boy wonder does it. My daughter gave him someone on a chain. Now the bowler starts his run up. An easy loping stride. At meals my daughter's boyfriend sits and touches it. I don't even think he knows he's doing it. He gets a kind of wistful look on his face and rubs his thumb across its soft surface. And then he sees her watching him and tucks it back inside his shirt. He looks down at his plate, his hair falls in front of his face and he disappears from sight the way his love token just has. Like a tortoise withdrawing into its shell. Now I'm watching the ball. Seam up. I'm watching his hand and the end of his tall, straight arm. I'm watching the ball again, which is coming at me faster than I expect. I'm thinking about the way his hair flows back to reveal his face. I'm thinking about his hands. I'm wondering what people mean when they say they're in love. Too late I realise the ball has left his hand. I take a big step forward but I'm a second – an eternity in cricket – too late. The ball cuts between my bat and pad and sends my middle stump cartwheeling across the grass.

'Got 'im,' says the guy in Hush Puppies.

'No luck, old man,' says the kid.

We lost, of course. Not badly, but still, a loss is a loss. All out with three runs needed. Rob undefeated somewhere in his forties. The changing room is a mess of sweaty clothes, frustration and deodorant. Nobody's happy with the outcome, but we also know it's early days. There's always next week. Rob comes through half dressed. He's in a hurry to get our match fees and head off for his date.

'You were batting OK,' he says. 'I was surprised to see you go.'

I shrug. I don't feel like talking. Over the years I've become used to getting out. I've learned not to mind so much because mostly I get caught and mostly it's my fault. But getting out to a good ball is different and, oddly, feels worse. Because, just when the team needed me to, I didn't pay enough attention.

'It's like your mind was elsewhere,' says Rob. 'What were you thinking?'

I LOVE…
Clearing the field

Let me take you back.

'Dad?' says my daughter.

'Yes?'

'You busy?'

'Not especially. Why?'

'No reason.'

'Oh, okay.'

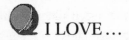

Of course I know that's not true. There's always a reason and sooner or later it will come out. Sooner or later she will judge the moment right and ask whatever it was she was going to ask. Could she do this? Could I pay for that? For the moment I smile and let it go. I like the fact that she calls me Dad. There were times, when she was small, when she experimented with my first name. Trying to sound grown up, I suppose. Trying to be one of the big people. She would roll it on her tongue the way she tried new foods, but, like spinach, she found it wanting and spat it out. She's older now, almost one of the big people. Entering a new phase. The third of Shakespeare's seven ages. An actor trying on new clothes. Like those repertory players in the theatre move between roles. Hamlet one day; Romeo the next. Today's too, too sullied flesh is forgotten in the sweet sorrow of tomorrow's parting. In real life it's not so easy. In real life we have our seven acts on the stage and we follow dutifully. One after the other, never to return. Mewl as a baby, whine like a schoolboy and sigh like the lover you hope to become. Do it like it's always the first time or always the last. And then move on, slipping pleasantly to nothingness.

'Dad?' she says.

'Yes?'

'Oh... nothing.'

'Oh, okay.'

If she's just about entering the third act, what about me? Shakespeare didn't say anything about men of a certain age gradually slipping down the pecking order of their cricket club's team sheets, but he would have had my number if he had. I suppose I am hovering somewhere short of the fifth age, the time of the justice 'in fair round belly', the time when 'desire doth outrun performance'. Just the inevitable consequence of slowing muscles and calcifying joints. Just what happens when you carry a few extra pounds around your midriff. Time was, I could play an off drive as elegantly and effectively as the next man. Time was, my brain said 'jump' and my body soared. Time was, I strolled down the beachfront and girls turned to look. Those were the days! Not any more. Nowadays my mind says 'run' and I walk. It says 'leap' and I fall. Nowadays I am more of what we in the cricketing fraternity call a mid-wicket specialist. Belting the ball is easy. You just swing your bat and see what happens. Playing a proper stroke is much harder. You've got to keep that elbow up. You've got to move your feet. You've got to keep your balance.

You've got, I suppose, to care. There are those cricketers who become fussier with age. They worry about their technique.

They throw a strop, the full double teapot with expletives undeleted, when they're given out leg before to a ball that in their view (though nobody else's) was going a yard down leg. They protest long and loud that the catch they were adjudged to have given was in fact nothing more than the ball brushing the top of their pad. Even though everyone on the field heard it. And the people in the Pavilion. And the deaf old guy buying tobacco three streets away. They stand at deep mid-on and practise cover drives that will never see the light of day. All that elbow high, front foot well forward, knee bent nonsense that goes out the window the minute a ball is bowled in anger. They study their averages and dream of the day when they will, once more, reach the halcyon heights of the season seven years ago when, three matches in a row, they were twelve not out at close of play.

'Um, Dad?'

The 'um' means she's getting serious. Probably going to ask for money.

'Yes?'

'Oh, um, nothing.'

And then there are people like me, those for whom the delight of leather on willow, of cream flannels against green, of the soft hum of bumblebees in the uncut outfield are the source of true delight. We don't much mind that our game is slowly, surely going to pot. We're not that fussed when some recently retired county circuit player smacks us over our head for three or four or five sixes in a row. We don't mind when an eight-foot teenage dynamo who's clearly not getting enough – or any – sex clatters us in the ribs three balls out of six before castling middle stump with the first ball of the next over.

Rob hates those guys. He's one of those players who practise their drives in the middle of the field. Difference is, he still has some prospect of playing them properly in the future. Although curiously he checks his drive. It becomes a kind of block-drive. When Flintoff does it, it goes for four between mid-off and extra cover. When I do it, it trickles out to point.

'These people should do more drugs,' I say when we meet between overs.

'How's the boy?' he asks. He knows me too well.

'Early days.' I say. He returns to practising his drives. I return to my end and wait for the teenage dynamo. In the field, players like me don't get all antsy each time we mis-field a spinning, cutting ball through mid-wicket. We applaud the shot and then trudge off to the boundary, whence we return the ball, underarm, to the bowler's end because it's closer.

But I digress. I was telling you about walking down the beachfront. I was pretending those were the days. Trouble is, they weren't. Because the girls would turn to look – and then what? Then every teenage anxiety would overcome me and I would trip over my own feet, landing face down in the remains of someone's forgotten ice cream. And the girls would turn their faces back to the sea or the sun or wherever they were facing before I was foolish enough to stroll by. That's the reality and if forced I can remember it all. But only if forced, because, despite all the evidence, every generation thinks it is the first. We reinvent our parents' lives and our children's lives and call them new. We pretend we are not like what has gone before and we fail to understand what is to come. Our parents did it and so will our children. Why should we be any different?

'Um, Daddy?'

'Um' and 'Daddy'? Both barrels, as it were, of the supplicant cannon. What? She wants to get her tongue pierced?

'Yes?'

'Is… is Mum in?'

Ah, the 'Mum' gambit. Well, that's a relief. Mum can deal with it. Whatever 'it' is.

'No.'

'Oh, okay.'

Except, when you think back, it somehow all feels familiar. Didn't we do this before? we ask. Doesn't this feel familiar? Not déjà vu exactly, but, well, not new either. Like something you saw in a movie once or read in a book. Like the first time you flew to the United States and felt as if you had been there already. Except you can't work out when it was, until you realise you saw it in the movies. Or maybe it was a story your father told you when you were young. The trouble is, you can't separate the characters from the names. You don't realise you're still in that repertory company, still touring. Still drinking cold tea in windy dressing rooms. Still fancying Ophelia, even though she's now a couple of years – decades – younger than you. Because now you no longer play the romantic lead. The blond kid, the one from RADA, has taken on Hamlet. Or Romeo. You're in the billing, but slipping down the rankings. Time was your name was up in lights. Well, not lights, but up there in large type anyway. Not now. You're more the Polonius figure these days, dispensing tired wisdom to an audience that doesn't listen and doesn't care. You could play Lear, I suppose, but frankly, who's got the energy? All that storming about. All that sound and fury signifying – well, you know what it signifies. And you know the worst part? The worst part is you watch the RADA kid and you realise he's better than you. Not better than you are now, but better than you ever were. The way, say, Nasser Hussain felt about Michael Vaughan. He has greater range, greater depth, greater appeal. And yet, somehow, there is this nagging sense that maybe, once, someone thought of you that way. Once upon a time you were the threat, even though you didn't realise it then.

And so here I am. Shakespeare's fourth age is the soldier. Not me. Not any more. Not with his strange oaths and beard. 'Sudden and quick in quarrel.' I'm not like that. Predictable and slow, that's me. I don't yell at the umpire, although I may still give the opposition a bit of lip. Tell them to walk when they might or might not have nicked one through to the keeper. That sort of thing. But mostly I shut up. Mostly I tell my teammates to let it go. I sound like someone's girlfriend on a troubled night out.

'Leave it, Rob,' I say. 'He's not worth it.'

And Rob may or may not leave it, depending on how bad his hangover is.

I am mellow now, you see. Not old, but older. I play bridge and do the crossword. I walk in the park and read large books beneath my favourite chestnut tree. I watch ducks with a new-found curiosity. I've developed an interest in gardening. Vegetables rather than flowers, but still – I have time to listen to things growing. You could say I'm at peace with the world. Sort of.

But then again, Shakespeare has his soldier 'seeking the bubble reputation, even in the cannon's mouth'. That might be me. Just a little. Despite my protestations above, I still do battle with the teenage dynamos. I still play league cricket. Lower league it's true. And lower order. But nonetheless it's competitive cricket. I still make a note of my season's batting average. It's only two or three seasons since I managed 46. OK, maybe four seasons. Or five. But I remember each ball. A golden summer that was. I remember the last innings. We played on the lovely ground in Highgate Woods in London, one of those public spaces where the batsmen should be – but never are – constrained by the presence of millions of children and toddlers playing football or eating ice creams at the edge of the field. The Corporation of London puts up signs warning patrons that cricket involves big blokes hitting a hard ball, but no one pays them any attention. Kids run on the field of play and there's invariably a gang of mums 'n' prams at cow corner. A target of sorts. That season I needed to make 80 not out in the final match to average 50 for the year. I didn't make it, of course. I was brought down by a vicious inswinging yorker that hit me on my big toe when I was on 43. Me and Don Bradman. Injudiciously (aren't they always injudicious?) given out LBW by my teammate – well, I won't name him; he knows who he is. A slow trudge back to the score box (Highgate Woods doesn't have a pavilion; you have to change in the shade of a passing oak) and a best ever season's average of 46.

Which is as good as it's got. Or ever likely to get as, season after season, desire doth outrun performance.

And I suppose I have to own up to other elements of Shakespeare's fourth age. The soldier is 'jealous in honour'. Me too, me too. I have daughters, you see, and I guard them jealously. Sorry about that. All I would say is that my jealousies pass as quickly as they arise. But then nor am I the 'slippered pantaloon' of the sixth age. Not quite. There are spectacles on my nose, it's true, and there are times when the world seems mad to me, mostly when some lager-fuelled lout is caught on tape beating old ladies and smacking policemen on the head only for his parents to appear on TV the next day to say, 'He's a good lad, really.' No, he bloody isn't. He's a lager-fuelled, misbegotten lout. See, I could audition for *Grumpy Old Men*; I hold the prejudices of the fifth age. I feel the same imminent fading of my once average powers. But no, I'm not old, not quite. Not yet. My voice is not 'reedy' and my 'shank is not shrunk'. Just the opposite. My shank, as my son might say, is well meaty. So let's say I am in the early stages of the fifth act. I am the justice, a youngish justice, a reasonably vigorous justice, 'full of wise saws' and with 'eyes severe'. I sit on boards and chair meetings. I have a house and a girlfriend and together we have children and a mortgage. When I fill in forms I admit that people are 'dependent' on me, even if they don't think of it that way.

Nor, to be honest, do I. At heart I play cricket. At heart I'm just a child.

What do you mean, that's coming soon? The final, seventh age of 'childishness and mere oblivion'? I said a child, not childish. There is a difference, you know. A child is wide-eyed and innocent. A child is happy. A child loves to play. But childish? Childish people need to be loved. Childish people need to win. Childish people think they matter more than other people. I'm not like that. Not at all. You'll see.

'Um, Dad,' says my daughter in the continued absence of my girlfriend, her mum.

'Yes?'

'You know you and Mum?'

I do.

'How did you, like, meet?'

Why is she asking me? Couldn't she wait to ask my girlfriend? She's the one who likes a late-night chat about feelings. She's the one who encouraged the kids to express themselves.

'How do you mean, "meet"?'

'You know, like, fall in love.'

'Oh, yes, well, that. It's a long story.'

'I have time.'

Damn.

'Well, we, um, we, well, like...'

'I mean, did you, like, know straight away?'

'Know?'

'You know, that she was the one?'

'Well, I don't know. Is she? I mean, it was... You know, well... Why?'

'No reason.'

Also not true. But like the answer to her question, I let it pass.

I LOVE …

Preparing the pitch

Not for long though. She was back the next day.

'Dad?'

'Yes?'

'You know my bed?'

I do. The one that creaks in the night. The one we bought her when she was too old for her cot. The one with stickers all over one end. The one she used to lie under at night and read books by torchlight because it made them more exciting. Even the ones with wizards and trains that leave from platforms that don't exist. That one?

'I need a new one.'

'Oh. Okay. I mean, why?'

'It's just not comfortable,' she says. She doesn't say for whom.

But I can't pay attention just at the moment. It's a Saturday morning in March and I have to get down to the club for a work party. There are things to be done. Leaves to be cleared. Grass to be mown. Pitches to be rolled. Trees to be trimmed.

'So can we get one?'

'Well, um, sure. I mean, not right now. Maybe…'

'Tomorrow?' The old pre-empt.

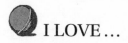

'Oh, okay, sure. I mean, tomorrow we can go and have a look.'

Like she hasn't already.

There's a guy in charge of the grounds at our club. We'll call him Dick. Dick is older than Solomon and wiser than any god. He has white hair, pursed lips and a schoolmasterly tolerance for the antics of the club's younger members. Of whom I am one, at least compared to Dick.

'I've only ever been wrong once,' he told me a couple of seasons ago. 'And that was about water.'

That's the way of conversations with Dick. You want to ask the follow-up question, but you also dread it. In what sense, you want to say, were you wrong about water? And was that really the only time? In all the 990 years you've been around? Weren't you wrong, for example, only last week when you gave me out LBW to a stinking ball that pitched a yard outside leg and should have been called a wide? Except that I nicked it, which means it couldn't have been a wide. But which also means I couldn't be out LBW. Were you not also wrong then?

But you're scared to ask, because goodness only knows what the answer might be. And before you ask, you want to be sure you want to know. I have a friend who works as a private detective. Divorce mostly. The great merry-go-round of north London love affairs. Who is sleeping with whom? 'And I'll tell you,' he said once, 'ninety per cent of my business. It comes from people who ask questions they really don't want to know the answer to. Like, "Is my wife having an affair?" Like, "Why does my husband smell like his secretary?" Because you think of hiring me,' my friend says, 'you already know the answer. All I do, I give them proof. Photos and *whaddafuck*? But a lot of people, they get the picture and they find, you know what, maybe they never want to know. So my advice, always, is be sure you want to know the truth. Because otherwise sometimes it turn round and bite you on the ass, you know what I mean?' My friend is Italian. He learned to say 'you know what I mean?' in about 1954 and has put it in every paragraph he's ever uttered since.

So I asked myself, did I want to know, if you know what I mean? And then I sighed. And then I asked. He probably would have told me anyway.

'How were you wrong about water?' It was a warm day. I settled lower on the bench by the outfield and closed my eyes to the sun. If he went on too long, I could always have a nap.

'Well, I wasn't really wrong,' said Dick. Dick is never *really* wrong, even about the only thing about which he was ever wrong. 'It was in the eighties and this guy said, he said, "Water's the thing." So I said, "What do you mean, water?" And he said, "People are going to start buying water. Do I want to put some money in it?" And I said no, because I thought, Water? No one is ever going to pay for water in a plastic bottle. I never thought anyone could be that stupid.'

Fortunately Joe comes by. He's got that amused look he gets. The one when he sees Dick has cornered some poor sucker in a conversation.

'Hey, Dick,' says Joe. 'When are we going to relay the pitch?'

Joe is one of the club's friendlier faces. He used to be our chairman, but he gave it up a couple of seasons back. Joe loves his cricket the way, well, the way I do. He loves everything about it. He'll sit for hours and watch nothing happening. Just the smell of mown grass makes his nostrils flare and his eyes dilate. Every club needs someone like Joe.

He opens the batting and he always makes a few. He'll field anywhere you ask him. He'll bake happily in 90-degree heat while the opposition flay our bowlers to all parts of the kingdom. He'll play in sleet and rain. He'll play in snow if you let him. He meets those twin impostors of victory and defeat with the same slow smile. He smooths ruffled feathers. He eases tensions. He volunteers to drop down a team when there are problems in the selection committee. He offers his car for away games. He remembers to thank the tea lady for the catering and he carries spare whites in his bag to lend to the guy – there's always one – who forgets his kit.

And he asks the difficult questions that no one else likes to ask.

Like when are we going to relay the pitch? The pitch is one of the things about which Dick has never been wrong. He's looked after this hallowed patch of turf since the Flood. And because of Dick, over the years the members of our club have grown to love the pitch. It's ours, it's different and there is even a case for saying it gives us an advantage. But they also know it can't go on for ever. They know that sooner or later things will need to change.

Because of the ridge. The ridge runs across one end of the entire square. Balls pitched just short of a length rear up and give catches to the slips. Fuller balls slide through at ankle height and hit the batsmen on the pads.

It's a complicated business, looking after a cricket pitch. The English Cricket Board even publish a book about it. Work starts at the end of each season. First there's what's called scari-fying, which is a process to remove any thatch and dead grass. Then you have to aerate the ground to help root development and nutrient uptake. Reseed the worn parts destroyed by overuse in the summer. And then the wicket ends need to be levelled before top dressing. Once the grass is growing, you can get rid of the weeds. And then leave it until March, which is what Dick does. And as a result our pitches are pretty good. Except for the ridge which has grown with each new layer of topsoil. Someday we're going to have to relay the pitch in its entirety. 'Pre-season rolling is absolutely crucial to the production of fast pitches,' says the ECB. 'The cricket square requires a firm, even surface and rolling should commence as soon as conditions permit. The groundsman is the only person who can decide when conditions are suitable.'[1]

'Hey, Dick,' says Joe. 'When are we going to relay the pitch?'

'Why?' says Dick.

'To get rid of the ridge,' says Joe. His brown eyes twinkle, but his face is serious.

'What ridge?' says Dick.

It's hard to argue with a man who is never wrong. Especially if he's the only person who can decide 'when conditions are suitable'.

Sunday morning. The showroom is buzzing with people looking at beds.

'Cos there's also a lump in my mattress,' says my daughter. 'It makes me lie all crooked and my back hurts.' The problem with the mattress is in addition to the problem with the bed. She needs a 'new everything'. Her words, not mine.

'Why this sudden interest in beds?' I ask. Sometimes I amaze even myself, how stupid I can be.

We're in a shop in Camden. If you live in London you'll know it. They advertise regularly. They have a list of celebrities who have bought their beds there. They source the wood ethically and make the beds themselves. They're good, strong, attractive and reasonably expensive. They're built to last.

And they're built for two.

I'm looking around for single beds. My daughter is curled up on what the catalogue calls a Sunday Double. It sounds nice and innocent, like a particularly rich and creamy dessert. It even manages to look nice and innocent, even though her burgundy death's head T-shirt looks like blood on the bed's white double thick Indian cotton duvet.

'This is the one you want?'

It is. She grins delightedly and bounces up and down to show me just how much. Her ratty old Converse trainers leave marks on the white duvet. She blushes and folds the duvet over so no one will notice. My guess is if we buy an £800 bed, no one will mind a couple of scuffs on a duvet.

I lie down next to her. My shoulders are a little stiff from the work party at the club the previous day. My thighs too. I got landed with the job of scrubbing the weeds out of the artificial pitch. Hard work, especially if the nearest you came to doing any exercise in the winter was three hours' Christmas shopping at Brent Cross. The bed is gorgeous and soft and welcoming. I stretch out on my back, fold my hands across my chest and close my eyes. It's so comfortable. It's just fantastic. I want to be there for ever.

'Dad! Wake up! Dad!'

There's someone holding my nose.

'You were snoring,' says my daughter.

I pretend never to have been asleep. I look around but no one seems to have noticed. So I sit up on the edge of the bed and look over at my daughter on the far side. She's waiting for me to say something. I shake my head to clear it and try to reassemble my thoughts. What was it we were talking about?

'Isn't it, you know, a bit big?' I ask.

She thinks I mean too big for her room at the top of our house, up in the rafters somewhere. At least I hope she does. The roof slopes steeply and I can only stand properly in the middle of the room. Which I won't be able to do if the space is taken up by a Sunday Double in oak satin finish with or without half-length underbed storage. She's smiling at me. I sigh. I guess we're going to have this conversation sometime. It might as well be now, in a crowded Sunday morning show-room.

'You really need, I mean, want, a bed this big?'

'Yes.'

She knows what I'm asking and she doesn't mind. I suppose she has also always known that sooner or later we would go through this.

'It's a nice bed.'

'I like the way the headboard slopes back.'

'It's certainly comfortable.' I resist the temptation to lie down again and curl into a foetal position. Instead I pretend to inspect the bed. Nice wood, good straight grain. Make a good bat, almost. Nicely finished. Sturdy construction. A quiet bed. A modest bed. A comfortable bed.

'Oh, okay,' I say.

She grins and then a flash of concern crosses her face.

'How will we get it up the stairs?'

'I think it probably comes flatpacked. They'll only assemble it once it's in your room.'

'Oh, okay. Can you take it apart again?'

'I guess so. It'll depend whether they use glue or not.'

'Cos you don't want to be stuck with something you don't like.'

No, no, you don't. I reach for my credit card.

'Thanks, Dad,' says my daughter.

I LOVE…

Reinventing the game

She was born in March, before the cricket season began. That morning Michael Henderson headlined his article in the *Guardian* 'Oh to be an Englishman now that April's here', even though it wasn't. His piece was about 'the end of the longest gestation period in modern cricket'. He meant the seven years it had taken Graeme Hick to become an England qualified batsman. Hick was – is! – an extraordinary and brilliant batsman. David Lloyd said it best, way back in 1991: 'I'm sick of watching him already. All he does is block the good balls and hit the bad 'uns for four.' When, finally, Hick did make it into the England team, his batting seemed to fall apart. I remember seeing him at the Cape Town Test match in 1996. England had made the usual hash of things in the first innings, but it was possible for them to redeem themselves second time around. Hick came in. He plonked Paul Adams, the young South African bowler, back over his head for a couple of towering sixes. Classic Hick shots. Simple, elegant and unbelievably powerful. I remember thinking two things. The first was, uh-oh, lost ball, as Hick drove high and deep so that from where I was sitting it seemed as if the ball must land on top of Devil's Peak. And the second was, There goes

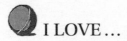

Adams's career. Hick was going to destroy him. No bowler can survive the kind of punishment that Hick was about to mete out.

But in fact Hick was soon out to a dodgy LBW decision off Pollock. He never really recovered after that tour. Adams had his moment in the sun and Hick became cemented in the public mind as a wonderful county player who never quite made it at international level.

Perhaps, like my daughter, he didn't want to be born. The labour lasted six hours, then twelve. Then eighteen and then 24. But eventually enough was enough. She popped into the world just before the *Today* programme's seven o'clock news (famine in the Sudan), then waited patiently while the nurses counted her toes and fingers (all present) and weighed her (9 lb something) and towelled off the mess that comes with birth. They handed her to my girlfriend, where she latched on to the breast like a desert rat downing a cold one in Alex while I stood and grinned like a demented banshee and wondered what the hell I had let myself in for.

'You okay, sweetie?' asked my girlfriend. I think she was worried about my tears, but actually I was fine. I was more than fine. I was the happiest man alive. I was flying. I was soaring and it was hard to imagine how or when or why I would ever come back to earth. I'll let you know when I do.

'And you?'

She was fine too. Apart from the pain and the fatigue and the day-and-a-bit of labour. And my damn fool questions in the night. And the fact that I may have nodded off when she most needed me. Apart from that, she was just fine.

There were details to be taken care of, but soon we were ready to go home. My girlfriend was finishing the paperwork;

I went ahead, cradling our hours-old daughter in my arms. I rounded the corner to see a young man about to hit the passenger window of our car with a brick. It was a brand new one. The car, not the brick. We had bought it especially for 'the baby'.

'I'm pregnant,' my girlfriend had said.

'We'd better get a decent car,' I had replied.

It was big and red and shiny and a marked improvement on the battered Mini that came before. I was about twenty yards away when I realised what was going on.

'Hey!' I yelled. 'Stop!'

He looked up, assessed the situation in an instant, and turned to face me, a feral belligerence in his stance. His left hand held the brick; his right hand was creeping towards a pocket that contained who knew what? A knife? A gun? A light for the cigarette dangling from the corner of his mouth?

'Why?' he said. 'What the fuck are you going to do about it?'

Good question. Took me by surprise, I admit, but there was no denying it. Tricky question. What the fuck *was* I going to do about it? Hmmm. Could you give me a moment there? I'm going to have to think about this one. Bit of a dilemma actually. New circumstances, you see. Everything was different now. In the past, before I had a daughter, I would have done the macho thing. Unless he was bigger than me in which case I would have run away. Or fallen asleep. I've done that too. Once, filming for the BBC in Soweto, we were being threatened by people who wanted to steal our rental car. They waved their gun in my face and demanded the keys and were rather taken aback when I hyperventilated for a moment, closed my eyes and fell asleep. My companion told me later that the conversation went like this:

'Is he dead?' said gangster number one.

'He will be,' said my companion. She was not the type to fall asleep merely because two young men were waving a gun in her face. She felt I wasn't pulling my weight in this particular scenario.

'Jesus,' said number one.

'What if he's dead?' said number two.

'They were worried that you'd had a heart attack,' my companion told me. 'No doubt they didn't want a murder rap hanging over them. Robbery was okay – but manslaughter? Not for the crappy car you had rented.' Actually the car was her choice, but we'll let that go. Because of the falling asleep thing. She deserves some leeway.

'Let's go,' said gangster number two.

'Give us your money,' said number one. Clearly the practical one.

'I don't have any,' said my companion. Also practical.

'What about him?'

'He' was snoring gently. A bubble of spit formed in the corner of his mouth. (I can't absolutely swear to this; I can only report what I've been told. You will have to decide for yourselves whether the witness was reliable.)

Gangster number one (or possibly two) swore loudly and unintelligibly. They looked at each other. And then they ran off. When they were about 50 metres away number one – or perhaps it was number two – turned and fired a shot in our direction. Well, in the air anyway. It missed us by miles – but the noise woke me up.

'Are they gone?' I asked.

I got no answer. My companion was tight-lipped and shaking and it was some time before she spoke again. When she did it was to say I was a yellow bastard and she hoped I would rot in hell. I'm sure she didn't mean it. A spur-of-the-moment thing. A whim. And ever since I have sworn by the theory that narcolepsy is the best defence.

But I couldn't go to sleep now. Not with my daughter in my arms. And anyway this guy was smaller than me. Scrawny. Ugly. And rude. Swearing in front of my daughter like that. But nor could I just dump her and fight him. I surveyed the street, a grey backwater in east London. There was no one around. I was, literally, helpless. I looked at him. He had that wiry quality of the undernourished class. But still, smaller and not as strong as me. He couldn't have been more than seventeen. The first flush of a moustache graced his upper lip. His hair was cut short, the kind of cut people have because it saves money, not because it is a fashion choice. His neck and cheeks were pocked with acne. His hand had emerged empty from his pocket. He had been looking for a light after all. In other circumstances I would have gone for it. But for my daughter I would have been running at him. I'm not a fighter, not by any stretch, but I was bigger and stronger than him and I would have fancied my chances. But these were not other circumstances. This was here, now, and I had to decide what to do. I had my daughter, I had my car and I had a problem.

We all tell ourselves stories. It's why I like fielding in the slips. There's a theory about close-catchers in cricket, about which ones should watch the ball from the bowler's hand and which ones should concentrate everything on watching the edge of the bat. If I'm not keeping wicket, I like to field at first slip. There for the misjudged shot, for the one where the batsman guards his off stump only to find the ball moves a little and comes off the edge. Low and hard and – with any luck – fatally to me. You have to pay attention, fielding at slip. You have, in that sporting phrase, to be 'in the game'. You have to expect the catch even though you know that of the 300 balls that will be bowled in an innings, only a couple – if that – will come to you as a catch. But you have to expect them to because when they do, you want to be sure to catch them.

As the bowler runs up I like to imagine the perfect catch. The ball pitches just short of a length. It moves a little in the air or off the seam. The batsman prods forward. The ball catches the edge and comes to me. And I pouch it. That's the key. In that instant, that brief moment of suspense from nick to catch, you know what to do.

'So,' said the spotted young man, 'you gonna fuck off or what?'

I hadn't, not in my wildest nightmares, imagined this. But then, strangely, I knew exactly what I was going to do. In some sense I was ready for it. His low blow held no terror for me. As long as he left my daughter alone, I was going to do nothing. And if I had been forced to articulate a reply to his questions about what the f*** I was going to do, it would have gone something like this. A fantasy answer, but an answer nonetheless:

'I'm going to tell you to help yourself. I am going to stand aside and watch. I am, in effect, going to do nothing. And I will tell you why. It's because between you and me and the lamppost I'm having an intense emotional experience right now and my daughter who does not yet have a name is more important to me than you or the car or the rest of the world will ever be. So help yourself to the car, take whatever you want. I recommend the Springsteen tapes you'll find in the cubbyhole. You will most likely find them more to your taste than Ella Fitzgerald.

'You might also want to take the tape deck. It will soon be obsolete, what with the CD revolution happening around us, but still. It must be worth something. The radio preset is tuned to Radio 4 long wave. For the cricket, you understand. The winter tours are my favourite. On late-night journeys you can immerse yourself completely in the cricket from Australia. Although to be honest this recent Ashes series has been a bit dismal. England thrashed. Well, we could live with that. It's not like it hasn't happened before. The really lousy part was the sense, particularly in the final Test, that they had given up. Sometimes it feels that way. Cricket's one of those games you've got to want to win. You can't just coast. Every ball, you have to say, this matters. I'm going to do everything I can to play it right. And in that game, it just didn't feel as if England cared enough. Not fair, I know, but there you go. Anyway, I like to listen to the radio.

'What's that? You don't care about cricket? Well, fair enough. Not everyone does. It's like poetry. You have to have invested a bit before you really enjoy it. You have to have put in the hours. Bone up on the grammar of it. Learn the words. Get into the narrative of it. Each match is a story, you see. But so is the whole game. A human story. A story of the twin impostors, triumph and disaster. A story of heroes and cowards. You could call it a romance. Playing cricket is like being in love. But I see you're not interested in that. Okay, no problem. Back to the car. I was saying you should help yourself. You're welcome, really. Because none of this really matters to me. The only thing that matters is my daughter.

'So you can take it all, but there is one thing. One small thing I should warn you about. In all fairness. And that is this: if you come near me, if you come anywhere near me, and therefore near my daughter (the one who is so young she does

not yet have a name but for whom I feel a love as deep and wide and intense as anything you will ever know), I will personally rip your throat out with my teeth. I will pluck out your eyeballs and tuck them in your nostrils. I will destroy...'

Maybe there was something in my face that completely betrayed what I was thinking. Some look of a wild animal guarding its young. Some hint of the extreme, bottled, protective violence I felt. He looked at me and I thought I recognised something in his face too. Not fear, exactly, but doubt. The recognition that he was dealing with something out of the ordinary. The suspicion of primal forces at work. He looked me up and down and took the stub of the cigarette from behind his mouth.

'Count yourself lucky, mate,' he said. He jerked a thumb at our car. 'Crap car anyway.'

Then he turned and sauntered away while I held my daughter and watched him go. I was strapping her into her new car seat when my girlfriend arrived.

'Let me look at her.' She pushed aside the swaddling gown to admire the scrunched red features of our daughter.

'She's beautiful,' I said. Typical English understatement.

'We should give her a name.'

'There's no hurry.'

'Everything alright?' she asked.

'Everything's just fine,' I replied. 'Everything's perfect.'

I LOVE . . .

Sharply rising balls

Fast-forward therefore to March 2007. I hear her calling from somewhere deep in the bowels of the house.

'Dad?'

'Yes?'

'Where are you?'

I am in the sitting room with her brother. We're following every twist in the saga of the Bob Woolmer murder. My son is twelve now and 'into' his cricket. But he is even more into murder. *CSI* will do that to a child. He has a book called *Forensics for Dummies* and, having read the first page, he regards himself as one of the world's leading pathologists.

'It had to be poison,' he says. 'Because of how they found the body.'

I am listening to a report on the Cricket World Cup. A week or so before, Bob Woolmer, the South African coach of the Pakistan team, was found dead in his hotel room. Now there is all sorts of speculation about why he died. Murder is a possibility. There are ugly rumours about asphyxiation. There is talk of bookies and deals reneged on and corruption in the game. Fingers are pointing every which way. It's a gripping drama, with all sorts of claim and counter-claim, fuelled by the death of a much loved man – and by the fact that nobody knows anything. It will later be shown that the rumours were false. Woolmer died of a heart attack. He was not murdered. But for now the intrigue and speculation is at fever pitch. The cricket world – not to be confused with the 'real' world – is awash with dark foreboding. The entire Pakistani team is under suspicion. The entire Pakistani nation has taken offence.

But I have another reason for my interest. It's a simple one: I met Bob Woolmer. I liked him. He coached me once, when I was a kid.

'You're kidding,' Rob said when I told him. 'You had coaching?' I wasn't paying attention and didn't see where this was going. So I nodded. 'You hide it well.'

Leaving that aside, it was the only professional coaching I've ever had. It only lasted half an hour, but to this day I do what he told me. He came to our school for an afternoon, sometime in the seventies. We all lined up to see him, uniformly tanned boys with sun-lightened hair, dressed in white T-shirts and white shorts. It was a hot afternoon and I remember how red his face was. A proper redneck, which was an Afrikaans term for Englishmen whose skins had not yet become used to the African sun. My father had been one once. I'm one now, when I go back there on holiday. When it was my turn in the nets, Woolmer stood behind and watched. John, a tall boy, was bowling short-pitched deliveries that came to me at about chest height. Because of the famous Englishman watching me (although in truth back then he wasn't famous – but he was foreign, which for us amounted to the same thing), I tried to play with a straight bat. A couple of times I managed to get bat on ball. A couple more times the ball shot past the handle of the bat and smacked me on the chest.

'Let me show you something,' said Woolmer. I stood behind him while he took guard.

'Same again,' he called to John.

John bowled. For Woolmer the ball was only waist high. He stepped back with his right foot and across his wicket, turned on his back foot and cracked the ball past where square leg would have been.

'Good shot, sir,' I said.

'It had nothing to do with the shot,' he said. 'What I had was good feet.' And then he showed me how to step back and across my stumps and to pull the ball through the on side.

'Because you're in no danger,' he said. 'The ball's not going to hit your wicket. It's too high. The worst that can happen is it's going to hit you. Big deal. If you don't want to get hit, don't play cricket. The point is, if the ball's not going to hit your wicket, you might as well score off it. And you can't do that by playing with a straight bat. Why? Because it's too high. So you have to pull it. But for that your feet have to be in the right place. It doesn't work if you don't move your feet. The key is to get back *and* across. Get behind it – and then belt it.'

I tried and missed. I was stepping back, but not across. It's not natural to go across your wicket because to do that is just to get more in the way of the ball. If a hard leather ball weighing five and a half ounces is coming at your ribs, your instinct is to run away, not to get more in the line of fire. Like a fencing coach, Woolmer made me put down the bat and practise just the step.

'Back and across,' Woolmer said, meaning step so that instead of hitting your hand, the ball is going to be heading straight for your heart. 'Back and across.' Together we did the move again and again, as if it was a dance class. It was Theodore Roethke's 'Waltz', only we were sober.

...I hung on like death:
Such waltzing was not easy.

Step back and across. Step back, across and turn. *One,* two three, *one*, two, three... Back, across and turn. And as you turn, you hit the ball. Our shadows did a puppet dance on the dusty pitch. The other boys were watching and I felt like the special one. And then I went back in the net. This time Woolmer himself bowled to me. A short ball, rising fast. The first one hit me just above the heart.

'Ow,' I said, but he was having none of it.

'Back and across,' he said. 'Come on, you can do it.'

He bowled again. I stepped back and across. I turned and pulled. And the ball sped from the bat like a bullet from the barrel of a gun.

'There you go,' he said with a smile. 'You got it?'

'Yes, sir.'

Cocky now, I invited him to bowl another.

'Go on, sir. As fast as you like.' He took me at my word and put his back into it a little more. I stepped back and across. I turned. I pulled... and the ball clattered into my ribs.

'Cricket only works,' he said, 'if you hit the ball.' His smile was a watermelon rind against the red flesh of his face.

'Dad?' says my daughter. It's her fourth go at the same conversation, the one she started the day before. She's wearing skinny jeans and a T-shirt. She has shoulder-length hair and a pretty dusting of freckles across her nose. She looks more like my girlfriend than like me. But you can see my side of the family too. I recently found a photograph of my father when he was that age. The spitting image, the pair of them. Long face. Sensitive mouth. Shy, curious, thoughtful eyes.

'Sure.'

'Will you be in later?'

'I guess.'

'Because there's someone I want you… I mean you should… I mean someone's coming.'

'Anyone special?'

She blushes. Were I a sleuth I would have said, 'Aha.' I know a clue when I see one.

'No,' she says. 'I mean, yes. I mean, not like special, special.'

'Oh, okay.'

'You know…'

I do. I do 'know'. She thinks I don't. She thinks I haven't noticed the traces of a young man about the house. The unidentified Vans trainers in the hall one afternoon. The fluffy pink heart that has materialised on her wall. Her sudden interest in skateboarding. At least, I assume she's interested. Why else would there be skateboarding magazines on the kitchen table? The text messages that ping suspiciously late at night.

'What was that?' we ask. 'Was that my phone? Who would be sending a text at this time of night?' But because it's late and because we all have phones, all five of us, the question of whose phone it was never really gets answered. Probably just some bloody telemarketing, we agree, and then forget about it.

Then there's the fact that she has dyed her hair black. Out of deference to what? Or whom?

The evidence is clear, but we have said nothing about the phantom boy in our house. But I know I will have to soon. I'm delighted the timing is hers, not mine. Because I have waltzed this waltz before, you see, back when I was a boy. I have known from the minute she was born that my time would come. But for the moment I'm not going to admit it. I am going to play dumb.

'What's her name?' I ask. How dumb can you get?

'Da-ad,' says my daughter. 'It's not a she.'

Aha! Another clue.

'A boy!' You can't accuse me of being slow.

'He's not a boy, Dad,' she says. 'He's a, he's a, well… he's...'

Let's just say for the moment that he lacks definition. I try to fill the silence.

'Did I ever tell you about my first girlfriend?' I ask.

She treats the question the way an uncertain batsman will treat a devious spin bowler. Imagine the scene. The ball has been given lots of air. Looping in over the wicket. It's going to pitch on a length. It may or may not turn. By rights the batsman should take two steps down the pitch and hit the ball 100 yards over mid-on. But, hmmm, you know what? It's hard to judge the flight of these little teasers. Hard to know where they're going to land. Hard to judge the turn. Will it be a ripper or one of those that comes straight on and gets him LBW? So he does nothing. He just pats it down into the pitch and waits for the next one.

My daughter declines the invitation to discuss my teenage love life. If you can call it that. She prefers fast bowling. Just say what you mean and get on with it. None of this messing around. None of this buying wickets with slow looping leg breaks. It's one of the easiest accusations to make against a batsman. 'Oh, he can't play spin,' they'll say in selection meetings. 'Doesn't have the footwork.' It may or may not be true; it's the worst kind of whisper because it's hard to refute. She purses her lips and looks at me.

'Oh, okay, well, sure. I'll be around,' I say. 'Look forward to meeting him.'

There's something else she wants to say, but I know she's not going to risk it either. She wants to say that I should be, you know, cool. Not cool in the happening sense. Just cool in a literal, please don't get excited, just, you know, be normal sense. But the moment passes and then there is nothing more to be said. My daughter and I specialise in such inconclusive conversations.

It's what makes us special, as in special, special.

I LOVE…

A measure of poetry

The boy's arrival ('He's not a boy; he's a, well…') coincides with the end of winter. The cold is bidding us a reluctant goodbye. Little flurries of sleet compete with the sun for our attention. The drab grey wasteland of our back garden is scarred with dabs of green. It is as though an artist is thinking of reusing the canvas. Perhaps he will try something else this year. A little brighter, and a little cheerier. A backdrop in shades of green. A study in bloom. Our garden is bordered on three sides by high walls. A triptych of shadow and light. A pallet of sandstone and grey. A painting of hope.

What was it Larkin said? The trees were coming into leaf, like something almost being said. Something like that. Spring as a whisper of things to come. Spring, the eternal promise. Spring and the sound of things growing. Being Larkin, of course, spring was the promise of death. Him and Eliot with his cruellest month. You're only born to die. There are no lilacs in our garden but there is lobelia and fuchsia, pansies and roses. There is a herb garden too. This year the coriander is growing particularly enthusiastically. It outstrips the parsley and the basil, the mint and the oregano. Even the rampant rosemary bushes seem tame by contrast.

Perhaps it is the wet spring. Perhaps it is the sun. I do not know. Spring in England always takes me by surprise. I have been here a quarter of a century but even now I am surprised by the speed at which things grow. By the *sound* of things growing. You can hear the vines, reaching out for the sun. I am surprised by the greenness. I am surprised by the abundance. I used to think this, my surprise, was a consequence of my roots. Where I came from nothing is ever this green. There is always an underlying brown. The red and brown earth is always pressing through the grass. But now I think it is more a question of the approach of middle age. I no longer expect to grow. I am surprised by renewal. I have crested the hill and am looking at the long, gentle slope on the other side.

It wasn't always that way, not for me, nor for anyone else. My daughter, for example, is in the springtime of her life. She is blessed by Eliot's desire without the attendant curse of memory. She is 'doing Larkin' at school. She doesn't like him. She doesn't like his ambivalence or the way he captures ugly thoughts in beautiful words. She doesn't like the essays she is asked to write. 'Larkin wrote, "Fear of death is too much of a screaming close-up to allow the poetic faculty to function properly, but demands expression by reason of its very frightfulness." To what extent would you agree that Larkin demonstrates these sentiments in his poetry?'

'What am I going to say?' she asks.

I'm in hands-off parenting mode. I alternate between over-attentive and hands-off, depending largely on whether I'm interested in what she's doing or not. I'm not that much of a Larkin fan either. I mean, some of it is quite nice. The 'trees coming into leaf' works for me. But all that misery stuff? Thanks but no thanks. And as for all that business about they fuck you up, your parents? Oh, please. You'll see. My taste veers more towards the inter-war crowd. Auden and MacNeice? Don't get me started.

'You'll think of something,' I say. 'I guess you have to decide what makes poetry good.'

She hesitates. Who can say what makes poetry good?

'I know what I like,' she says.

'That's a good place to start.'

I have every confidence. My daughter is an old hand at this game. She opts immediately for 'a bit of both' because she knows that will please the teacher. She throws in a quote or two. She uses phrases like 'on the other hand' and words like 'nevertheless'. Larkin's lines 'demonstrate', 'illustrate' and 'suggest'. And (without ever offering a view of what makes poetry good) she concludes that Larkin was talking hogwash. His self-assessment was wrong. His fear of death does not for a second impede his ability to write poetry. It's just one of those things he liked to complain about. A bit of a moaner, our Larkin. A bit of a whinger. A miserable old man – and all three of those, miserable, old and man, are meant as pejorative.

And nothing, really, to do with her.

For my daughter has grown up in a visual age. In her world memory is not words on the page but the photo montage on her bedroom wall. It shows holidays mostly. There are blue lakes and yellow hills. There are trout streams in the Drakensberg and chestnut groves in Tuscany. The white frozen lakes of Pennsylvania echo the pale beaches of the Peloponnese. There are photographs of her brother and sister, of my girlfriend and me. We seem always to be laughing. A wonderful catalogue of elision. There are no tears in the photographs and no tantrums. There are no worries. There are no deaths and no decay. There is a family tree going back three generations. At the top are the three children. Then my girlfriend and me. Then our parents. Her wall of memories is like an advertisement for one version of a television-commercial life. A Pollyanna wall, where everything is for the best in the best of all possible worlds. Happy parents, smiling kids. What's not to like?

Even I haven't changed that much over the decade and a half since she was born. A little balder, perhaps, and such hair as there is is white rather than grey. My glasses are a little more fashionable. My body – well, not that much different. A little heavier, perhaps, but not alarmingly so. A little less upright. A little less fluid. I don't have that athletic – what's the word? – grace. That sense that I can run and leap and dance for ever. The sense that movement is my default position. The feeling that there is no time lag between the instruction that comes from the brain and the action that follows in the body. I have become a lake rather than a stream. I no longer flow the way I used to. For when I look at it again there is something sedentary about the set of my shoulders. Something introverted. Something bookish. Something, well, disappointing.

Except for one. One picture I like. It shows me on the pull and, no, I don't mean in a bar in the West End. I mean in a picturesque little village on the border between Essex and Hertfordshire where my club plays an annual cricket match. I mean doing what Bob Woolmer taught me 30 years before. The pitch is laid in the middle of the village green. Beyond the modest clubhouse are fields of wheat and rape. On the other side a B road so minor it features only on the most detailed maps winds through houses set far apart. Beyond mid-wicket there is a thatched pub where they sell sandwiches the size of shoeboxes. At fine leg a cow ponders the passing parade. It has all the time in the world to 'stand and stare'. The fixture happens every year in late July, by which time, even in the wet summer of 2007, the pitch is hard and firm and true. A batsman's pitch. Our matches there are usually high-scoring affairs. Three of my top five scores have come on that pitch. Partly because it is hard and true. And partly because the square leg boundary is only 25 yards away. Mis-hits go for six. Proper shots get lost in the wheat. At the end of each season the farmer harvests any number of balls, some as good as new.

The photograph is taken from behind, so you can't see my face. You can see Rob down the other end. He's got that, 'Oh God, Sandy's going to get himself out' look on his face. The one he gets when I am at the crease, we're nine wickets down, and we need five runs to win. What you can also see is that 30 years on, my back foot, my right foot, is 'back and across'. Very good. Admirable technique. I am doing a Woolmer and the old master coach would have approved. Especially if he had seen me recently. Not often these days you see me moving my feet. Not since I was stumped three matches in a row hop-skipping down the pitch to a series of legside pie-chuckers. In the photograph my weight is on my back leg even as I swivel to pull the ball over square leg. My wrists are firm. I am in control of the shot. This is my homage to Bob Woolmer. No mis-hit, this. It's going into the wheat and beyond. A lost ball for sure. Square leg is looking up at the ball. His hands are raised for the catch that will never come. For a split second before I connect with the ball he must have thought, Hold on, this is coming my way. But then I hit it with the sweet spot in my bat and it flew, high and wide, as free as a bird. His hands remain where they were, ready for the catch, but his face tells a different story. His eyes are rolling back in his head, trying to keep up with the ball flying overhead. His jaw has slackened just a little or perhaps he is framing a word. A curse or a gasp – I don't mind which. Either is appropriate. The bowler is not in the picture but I can tell you what he looks like too. He is a man of a certain age, as am I. He has been playing village cricket for, say, 35 maybe 40 years. He has kept in shape, but each season it costs him that little bit more to bowl ten overs. In the old days he beat people for pace. Nowadays he has to rely more on guile. The fast ball rising sharply outside off stump won't do it any more. Nowadays he uses a whole new range of words to describe the act of dismissing batsmen. He 'winkles' them out. He 'tempts them into something rash'. He 'nags away' just short of a length. And mostly he does it well. His bowling figures are still respectable. The team captain doesn't mind tossing him the ball. He doesn't have to send the selection committee one of those embarrassing e-mails trumpeting the success of two or three or four summers before. He doesn't have to call up the glories of some long-forgotten rout, played on a pitch where the top score was eight and that only because the number eleven managed to snick his first two balls through the slip cordon before being clean bowled by the third ball, to justify his place in the team. He is not, yet, resting on his laurels.

But he is getting on. And so sometimes his ball-just-short-of-a-length becomes a rank long hop – and when that happens ageing brutes like myself, men whose natural eye for the ball can just about compensate for their diminishing pool of technique, swat him over the boundary for six. And so there he is, standing a little way down the pitch, sweating like a pig, his hands on hips and his mouth in a disgusted pout while I swivel on my back foot and plant his ball 40 yards back into the wheat field. Not that I care what he looks like.

It was a lousy ball and I hit it for six. It got what it deserved and any degree of humiliation, disgust, embarrassment, frustration or rage experienced by the bowler only adds to the pleasure of the shot.

Plus someone took the picture. I must remember to thank him.

It's sweet of my daughter to have it on her wall. She doesn't care for cricket but she knows I do. I suspect she thinks it has comic value. There is something slightly exaggerated about the way my flannels hang from my backside and for people who don't understand the shot it looks as though I am off balance although in fact I am perfectly placed. I will continue to swivel, plant my left foot on the ground and recover in time to see the ball land. The ball, by the way, is visible in the picture, which is partly what makes it such a nice one. It has travelled perhaps twenty feet and it is still rising. There is no doubt about where it is going.

But perhaps she does not have it there for comic value. None of the other pictures are meant as jokes. They are pictures of us in happy times. So perhaps she really does think this captures some essence of me, some forgotten detail that would not emerge, say, from a picture of me doing my imitation of a beached whale on a Mediterranean beach, or me in typical pose, asleep on the sofa with an improbable tome slipping unread down my chest. Her bedroom is next to my study and I heard her once describing the picture to a friend from her new school. 'Oh, that's my dad,' she said. 'He thinks he can play cricket.'

Well, no doubt you can parse that little sentence for yourself and share, for a moment, the mild insult of 'thinks'. But things improved:

'Mine too,' said her friend.

'Yeah, but mine actually can,' said my daughter. I knew

there was a reason I loved her. 'Or he says he can. I mean, I've never actually watched him.'

Did I say 'love her'? I must have been thinking about something else.

The key, of course, is in the confession. 'I have never actually watched him.' And why should she? We live in inner London where, Lord's notwithstanding, cricket fields are as rare as trout streams. You can find them if you try, just as you can catch trout if you really put your mind to it. But they are not the essence of the city in the way that, say, they are the essence of villages that lie on the Hertfordshire/Essex border, surrounded by wheat and rape with nothing louder than the crack of leather on willow to disturb their bucolic charm. There are many things we do together, but cricket is not one of them. Walking, hiking, cycling. We climb rocks and we go running. She did her Duke of Edinburgh award recently and one of the requirements was a certain amount of exercise per week. Which was why, through the long winter just passed, she dragged me twice a week from my pre-dawn bed to go running across the icy black paths of Hampstead Heath. My fault really. I taught her the supposed virtues of the early-morning run when she was thirteen. We were going to 'do' Kilimanjaro together and even I accepted that this would require a modicum of training. But finding mountains in central London is even harder than finding cricket grounds and we had to make do with running our way over Hampstead Heath and Alexandra Palace, which were as good as it got.

But cricket?

'I think not,' she said.

We've talked about it before, but she's not interested. Not her thing. She doesn't much like sport and she definitely doesn't like ball sports. And now, as March gives way to April,

I wonder whether I should return to the fray. Perhaps this season she might be interested in cricket? Perhaps she will catch a glimpse of some bronzed Australian on the television, or one of the new young players from the West Indies. Perhaps Chanderpaul's baseball make-up (he smears some black stripes under his eyes before he goes to bat) will take her fancy. God help us, she might even fall for all the hoopla surrounding England's latest boy wonder, the South African prodigy, Kevin Pietersen.

I float the idea at dinner one night. A seamless gear shift from Larkin's poetry to the joys of cricket.

'Cricket is like poetry,' I say.

'Yeah, right,' says my daughter.

Actually, the thought is not mine. I show her a piece in *The Times* by Ben Macintyre in which he argues that cricket, of all sports, lends itself to poetry: 'This is a sport measured out in metre and stanzas, in line and length. Every over is a verse. Every innings is a poem: sometimes an epic, sometimes merely a haiku… Above all, cricket furnishes the time necessary for poetry: not 90 minutes of crammed action, but five full days in which to assemble thoughts in verse, ball by ball, line by line.'

'You're kidding, right?' says my daughter. 'They'd fail me if I tried that in an essay.'

Well, maybe they would. But I like to think Macintyre's right. Cricket and poetry do go together. The MCC has just brought out an anthology of cricket verse. All 450 pages of it. Could football match that? Or rugby? Or any other sport you care to name. Baseball, I suppose, if you're American or Cuban or Japanese. In his foreword to the anthology, Tim Rice puts it clearly enough: 'Cricket literature has no equal in sport.' Byron, Keats, Wodehouse, Hughes, Betjeman, Masefield, Housman, Wordsworth. And, perhaps, most famously, Henry Newbolt, who leaps in the flash of a pentameter from every playing field in every village, to the dread battlefields of war where England's sons face a challenge of a different order. The response, though, is the same. Whether seeking victory in a tight game, or taking on the enemy with death all around, the 'Gatling jammed' and the regiment 'blind with dust and smoke': 'Play up! Play up! And play the game!'

Will the affinity of cricket and poetry remain unsullied? Will Macintyre's claim be true next year? Or the year after? For what seems like years now the world of cricket is in something approaching turmoil. It is possible still to drift down to Lord's on a Sunday and watch a soporific, rain-interrupted, Duckworth-Lewis[1], only 1,500 spectators and half of them are asleep match between, say, Middlesex and Kent. But six hours and a world away the stars of the Indian Premier League are creating a new and different game and four hours in the other direction Sir Allen Stanford is waving unimaginable millions at the game.

I do not know. But I do know the peace of a slow day at Lord's. I do know the gentle rhythms of cricket. Which is not to say that cricket is a gentle game. But it has a gentility. This is not about the MCC and its famed attempts to formulate the 'spirit' of cricket. The 'spirit' was introduced as a preamble

[1] The Duckworth-Lewis method is a mathematical model used to calculate the target score for the team batting second in a cricket match interrupted by weather or other circumstance. It is widely accepted as fair, but is not without controversy because it attempts to 'predict' what would have happened. The essence of the 'D/L method' is 'resources': the number of overs they have to receive and the number of wickets they have in hand. At any point in any innings, a team's ability to score more runs depends on the combination of these two factors and the 'result' is calculated accordingly

to the 2000 edition of the Laws of Cricket and suggests that 'cricket is a game that owes much of its unique appeal to the fact that it should be played not only within its Laws but also within the Spirit of the Game. Any action which is seen to abuse this spirit causes injury to the game itself.' Responsibility for the spirit – which means RESPECT (in capital letters) especially for umpires and opponents – rests largely with the two captains. In my experience some captains take this seriously. At my club one of the better teams has a captain for whom the spirit is paramount. Sometimes I play for him. Usually during a cholera outbreak, or in August when everyone else is on holiday. Recently, after a fractious and unpleasant game, during which the 'spirit' was conspicuous by its absence, he locked us in the changing room and gave us a dressing down. Curious to see the pumped-up, adrenaline-fuelled, macho nonsense of the previous hour wilt and fade like winter leaves. Curious to know that there remains, within the game, a kinship with the poetic impulse. I know the ripple of applause that greets a failed batsman as he trudges back to the pavilion. I even know the enthusiastic cheering that greets a successful one.

But my daughter is having none of it, not even on the many occasions I invite her to come with me to Lord's. Not even when I talk about the beauty of the game. Its rhymes and its rhythms. Or even the beauty of its practitioners. She gets the giggles at the thought, though whether this is because she finds the idea of Lord's or the idea of cricketers as fantasy objects ridiculous remains unclear. And besides, she has a fantasy object of her own. And he's coming to dinner. But that's okay. I'm ready for this. I've been here before.

I LOVE ...

Playing the Bradman card

South Africa, 1976

Her name was Annie and her eyes were grey. She had a pretty nose, small hands and a father the size of Texas. He looked like a volcano about to erupt. The hair on his shoulders sprouted like flames above his collar. His eyebrows met in the middle and his hands were like baseball mitts. He appeared to have no neck and he had borrowed his chest from a passing rhino. And his skin, for that matter. It was burned to a dark copper and lightly dusted with the pallid grey sheen of a heavy smoker. Even now a cigarette burned in his hand. I doubt he knew it was there. Not that I planned to ask. I was nearly fifteen years old and he was the scariest thing I had ever seen.

'Bat or bowl?' he growled. He didn't bother to ask whether I played. What sort of boy didn't?

'Bat,' I said. I was about to say 'or bowl'. It seemed better to hedge my bets, even though I couldn't bowl for toffee. But he was already stalking down the pitch to put the wickets in at the other end. It wasn't an actual pitch, of course. It was a strip of lawn that ran between the swimming pool and the endless sugar cane that covered the hills for miles around. But when I looked at it more closely I could see it had been mown and rolled more than the rest of the lawn. A cricket pitch, in the middle of his garden. What kind of lunatic...?

'You'll be with me,' he said.

'Lucky you,' said Annie. A flutter of concern creased her brow. 'You can bat, can't you?'

'Course,' I said. 'Of course I can.'

Which was a matter of some doubt. It had been a while since I'd played at all. A year or two before I had lost interest in cricket. It was after I injured myself in a freak accident one hot summer afternoon just before Christmas. I had sliced through my Achilles tendon. There was a loud snap as the muscles of my calf bolted for the safety of my knee. I remember the cramp most of all. There was hardly any blood. 'A small wound, but a lot of damage,' the nurse said. She arranged some mirrors so I could watch the doctor sew it back together. I was in a cast for months and on crutches even longer and by the time it was finished my interests had mostly shifted to books. Books and girls, though not necessarily in that order. There had been plenty of books, but girls? You were more likely to find water in the Kalahari than a girl on my arm.

Until Annie.

We had spent the day at the beach with friends. We were the two reading books. She had invited me – 'It'll just be us' – back to the farm for supper. But after that we could, you know, entertain ourselves.

Just us, my foot. Her father took one look at me and announced we had 'enough' for a game of cricket. At the far end of the pitch he was allocating players. Annie, her brother, her brother's friend Fred and the dog formed one team. Her father, her younger sister Liz and me the other.

'You gonna play, doll?' he said.

'Doll' was Annie's mother. But she was on her third martini

and wasn't 'gonna' play anything. Annie's parents may not have known it then but they were working their way to a messy divorce. He had fallen for the bottle blonde from Amanzimtoti. Doll had settled for the bottle. There was no way back for either of them.

We had a huddle, just like the pros do.

'So listen, you,' he said. He meant me. 'Annie's okay and her brother also. Not hopeless, if you know what I mean. Fred, not so much. You?'

'Me?'

'You any good?'

'Well, I mean, I don't...'

'It's a simple question.'

'Yes,' I said. Suddenly defiant. I was 'any' good.

'We're gonna bowl first, okay. You, you field on the on side. Liz on the off. I'll bowl straight so we don't need a keeper.'

We broke the huddle. It was like coming up for air. I felt as if I had smoked three cigarettes while I was down there. Perhaps I had. He was lighting a new one.

'Okay, let's toss,' he said. He reached into his pocket for a coin and flipped it in the air.

'Heads,' called Annie. The coin disappeared into her father's vast hand.

'Tails,' he said without looking. 'We'll bowl.'

They had done this before. Annie opened the batting with Fred. Her old man bowled. Annie played forward defensive. Technically correct in every respect. The ball trickled out to Liz and there was no run. Second ball the same. And the third.

'How long are we playing?' said Annie's brother.

'Shut up, Carl,' said Annie. I made a note of his name. Should I ever need it. They weren't much of a family for introductions.

'As long as it takes,' growled his father. He got ready to bowl again.

'Don't let him talk about cricket,' Annie had warned me as we walked up the drive.

'Why not?'

'Believe me. It's not worth it. He only does it to… to…'

I didn't press her. I wasn't much interested in her father or cricket or what he did it to… to… I was interested in our first kiss, which all the signs suggested was imminent.

'So you promise?' she asked.

'Sure,' I said. 'I promise. No cricket.'

Like I had a choice. Her father bowled. A little short, a little wide. Annie gave herself a little room and cut it sweetly into the swimming pool.

'Six!' yelped Carl in delight. One look from his old man shut him up.

'You sure it wasn't a catch?' he said to Liz. Liz ignored him. He might have scared me, but he didn't seem to scare his daughters. The dog retrieved the ball from the pool. Annie looked at me.

'You would have caught it, right?'

'Course.'

'Yeah, right.'

Next ball, also short on middle stump. Annie stepped inside and pulled it. Hard. Low. Fast… and straight at me.

'Catch!' yelled Liz.

'Drop it!' yelled Annie.

Neither of these were in my gift. The ball hit me in the stomach, bounced off my arm and nestled in my armpit.

'Howzat?' I said gingerly.

'Jesus Christ,' said her father. 'I hope you bat better than you field.'

I did. With Annie out, the two boys put on 32 runs before Carl was clean bowled behind his legs. Our turn to bat. Fred clearly had a crush on Liz. He was bouncing around his mark like a bull moose in the rut while she took guard. Then he ran up, bowled at something like 300 miles an hour and sent her middle stump cartwheeling onto the barbecue area by the French windows. She pretended to hit him and he pretended to be hurt. Young love. I caught Annie looking at me and smiled.

'Hey, you,' said her father. 'New boy? You're in.'

Fred didn't seem to have a crush on me. His next ball was slower, wider and shorter. I cracked it past Carl's ear into the pool. Six runs. Annie's father was pulling on his cigarette at the time. He dissolved into a fit of coughing. I thought he might die.

'That's his way of saying nice shot,' said Annie.

The dog fetched the ball and we won without further trouble.

'That's the last time you catch me,' said Annie. She play-slapped me on the cheek and ran behind the house. With a quick glance at her father (he was busy pulling up the stumps), I gave chase...

I caught her several hours later, when we had done the washing up.

'You don't play cricket?' her father had asked at dinner. Annie rolled her eyes. Her mother refreshed her drink. Light glanced off her eye shadow like shards of glass.

'No, sir,' I replied. 'Not really.'

'So what do you do?'

I couldn't even offer him rugby. I had given that up as well, even before I got injured. I didn't mind getting hit by a cricket ball but I did mind getting hit by Afrikaner boys who were three times bigger and ten times tougher than me. What else could I say? I didn't even bother with books. I knew they would get short shrift. I offered him tennis, but he showed a glimmer of interest only when I mentioned hockey. A proper game, with a proper hard ball, I suppose.

Annie was giving me a funny look over the top of her glasses. The conversation moved on. To the weather. To the price of sugar. To the new stamps the government had brought out. They were doing flowers that year. Proteas, I think. My grandfather was a modest philatelist.

Her father took the gap. 'Stamps are all right,' he said. 'If you like that sort of thing. But me? I prefer cigarette cards. I've got cigarette cards from way back. I've got cards that when you sell them, you're gonna get a lot of dough. A lot of dough. You want to see them?' I shrugged. He went to his den to find them.

Annie shook her head. 'What are you doing?' she hissed.

'What could I say?'

'Jesus.'

'Got them,' said her father. He laid the cards on the table in front of us. They were old ones he had inherited from his father. They showed cricketers I had never heard of. Black and white pictures of men with chiselled jaws and slicked-back hair. Below the names were their counties and countries and their career statistics. But the one he most wanted me to see was missing.

'Shit (pardon my French),' he said. 'Where is it? I know I had it. He was the greatest, you know.'

He meant Don Bradman. Back then I had heard of Bradman, but I didn't know anything more about him. He was just a name. But Annie's father 'knew' him and said he was the greatest player there ever was. Or ever would be. 'I saw him, hey,' he said. 'I saw him at the Oval in 1948. The guy needs just a few runs, like a handful or something, to average a hundred in tests. Can you imagine that?'

I couldn't. But with a surreptitious glance at Annie, I nodded.

Her father's memory seemed to have hardened.

'Four runs he needs. Four! He gets four and his Test average is one hundred. But he was bowled first ball. I don't know, maybe it was second ball. Out for a duck and his average is 99.94. Can you imagine? Every time this guy goes in they expect him to make a hundred. He expects to make a hundred. Jeepers, he was some guy.'

I nodded.

'You know what it is to make a hundred?'

Actually I didn't. Top score ever was 72. But I nodded anyway.

'So you want to see the card?'

Another glance at Annie. She was shaking her head again.

'Sure, I mean, I guess. Yes, thank you, sir,' I said.

The old man was smiling at me or maybe he was smiling to himself. I couldn't see his eyes to tell.

'Cos this guy was something else.'

'Yes, sir.'

'So you gotta see him.'

'Thank you.'

'I know it's somewhere,' he said, scratching through his album. 'I had it out just the other week. You seen it, doll?'

Doll wasn't in much of a state to see anything. She hiccoughed and the conversation died. An uncomfortable silence filled the room. On the radio Bonnie Tyler sang: 'It's a heartache, nothing but a heartache…'

It was quite late by the time Annie and I escaped to the garden.

'We're just going outside, Daddy,' said Annie. 'We'll be down by the swing.'

'Okay, angel. Don't do anything I wouldn't do,' growled her father. His voice was like car tyres on gravel.

'We won't.'

Damn. I was all for doing things her father wouldn't do.

Turned out she was fibbing. Or maybe he would do them. Maybe he already was with the lady from Amanzimtoti. Across the valley the dogs barked in endless rounds. A breeze ruffled the bougainvillaea by the pool. Debby Boone replaced Bonnie Tyler. 'You light up my life, you give me hope…' Beyond us the green wall of sugar cane stood sentry against the night sky. We lay on the grass and looked at the stars. I pretended to know their names and Annie pretended to care.

'Beetle Juice?' she said. 'Now you're talking shit.'

'True,' I said. 'Look! You can see it's redder than the others. So the old guys, they thought it had the blood of lots of bugs. So they called it Beetle Juice.'

'And the others? What did you say they were?'

'The twins, Castro and Pollock,' I said. The names tripped off my tongue as lightly as anything.

'What, like the cricket guy?'

She meant Graeme Pollock, the South African batsman. So, probably, did I.

'Well, I don't think they named it after him or anything. I mean, he came later. But, *ja*, just like that.'

'Is that a fact?' she said. She didn't mean it as a question. It was just a habit of speech. Something she had learned from her old man. A way to fill in the spaces.

Even so, a space appeared.

I thought I could probably fill it. Me and the Bee Gees. 'How deep is your love (is your love?), I really need to learn…' Their distant voices were thin on the evening breeze. I propped myself up on one elbow and pointed to the sky.

'And you see that one over there?' I said.

To make sure she was lining it up right, I put my head right next to hers. I heard her lips open with the faintest pop of parting saliva. I could smell her sherry trifle breath and feel the soft downiness of her skin.

'You see there,' I said. 'The cross, the one that looks like a cross. You can use that to get to the South Pole.'

The South Pole. A sort of celestial version of third base.

'What, all the way?' she asked. You bet all the way. At least I hope so. I mean, that's why we're here, isn't it? Although if truth be told, the prospect of 'all the way' scared me silly.

'I mean not, like, to travel there,' I said. 'You've still got to sail or something. But, like, to know where you're going.' I wished I knew a little more about where I was going.

'Is it?' Another phrase from her old man. A variation on 'Is that a fact?'

'There's like a maths thing you've got to do. You take an imaginary line from the middle…'

She didn't say anything. She may have been thinking about our feet. About the way they were touching so lightly. Maybe she had the same intense pain – or was it pleasure? – in the small of her back. Perhaps she too felt her clothes constrict in unexpected places. This polar exploration was harder than I thought.

'You take this imaginary line from… from…'

There was an all-too-real line taking shape in my trousers. I bent my body to keep that part from touching her. It seemed the polite thing to do. But I kept our faces close. I felt her eyelash brush mine. I turned to look at her. She had taken off her glasses.

'You can stop pointing,' she said.

'Oh, sorry.' I moved my groin further away.

'No, you idiot. Your arm.'

She giggled. I smiled. I let my arm fall. From the stars to heaven in the blink of an eye. It fell all the way from the Southern Cross to her right breast. I didn't know where else to put it, so I left it there. There was a button and I fiddled with it. She shifted a little.

I stopped. 'Sorry,' I said.

'No, I like it,' she said. She grabbed my wrist and pulled my hand back to the spot. I groped around for the button. It wasn't a button at all.

'You can kiss me now,' she said.

'Okay.'

Which was not how I felt. My mouth was dry. My hands were clammy. My back hurt, there was a stone digging into my hip and my groin felt like someone had lit a small fire there. But there was no turning back now. It was time to shut up and pucker. I closed my eyes and leaned forward.

'Hey! Hey, Annie. Yoo-hoo, An-nie!'

The yell came from the house. There was no mistaking her father's tobacco-stained voice. 'Hey, Annie! I found it. Is that guy, whatshisface, still with you? Come on up to the house. There's something I've gotta show him. I've got the Bradman card. It was on the mantelpiece.'

I sighed. Possibly with relief.

'Oh, shit,' said Annie. 'He put it there the last time.'

The *last time*? It took me twenty-five years to work out what she meant. I wonder who the guy, old *whatshisface*, was that time?

Rob looks alarmed when I tell him this story. He is still young enough to be interested in other people's daughters (although too old to be interested in mine).

'Jesus,' he says. 'So did you two ever get it together? After that, I mean? I mean, Jesus.'

He shakes his head in terror at the prospect of playing cricket with the father of a future object of his affections.

Well, no, Annie and I never did get it together. The moment had passed, just as her father intended, and it never reappeared. There were bumbling apologies, a quick goodbye and a long walk through the night back to my campsite at the beach. I remember the house and trees and the yellow light from the living-room window. I can see her mother's red nails clinking on the whisky glass in which she drowned her loneliness and the gun rack above the bar. I can bring to mind the smell of burning wood on the wind and the sound of rats in the sugar cane. I can feel her dress and my shirt, and the soft touch of her fluttering eyelashes on mine.

But most of all I remember her father and the way he played the Bradman card. In cricket they say that timing is everything. You sure as hell couldn't fault him on that. His timing was perfect, as sweet and unanswerable as a straight drive from Michael Vaughan.

'You don't even watch cricket?' he had asked as we looked at the photograph of Bradman and that magical, incredible 99 and a bit Test average.

Dangerous ground again. I had when I was younger. I still followed it in the papers and on the radio. That afternoon

Allan Lamb had made a century at Kingsmead in Durban, playing for Western Province against Natal. But I hadn't been to a match for a while. When I was younger a friend and I would go to Kingsmead and collect autographs. That was the time of the South African greats. Barry Richards and Mike Procter, Eddie Barlow and Graeme Pollock. The gentle and forgotten giant, Vince van der Bijl. I got Procter's signature nineteen times. A school record.

'I used to,' I said. 'But now...'

'Too much schoolwork, hey?'

'I guess.'

'Don't worry about it. You'll come back to it.'

'I'm not sure...'

'Cricket's a funny game. Once it's got you, it's never going to let you go.'

I LOVE…

The reverse sweep

A bit early, I know, to be playing the reverse sweep. It's the sort of shot you should save for later in the innings. When you've got your eye in and when the bowlers are getting tired. When the need to get runs is greater than the need to preserve your wicket. But ask anyone at my club. They will tell you that getting my eye in is not my strong point. I am not known for my patience. None of that nurdling for a few overs before I start playing my shots. And, anyway, sometimes an early reverse sweep works. Take the bowlers by surprise, upset them early on, and maybe they'll bowl badly as a result. It's very hard for the bowler to find his line if he thinks that at any moment you're going to hit him in the wrong direction.

My girlfriend finds me in the kitchen.

'She's got a boy,' she says.

'"Boy" as in "boy"?' I ask.

'Yes.'

'Have you seen him?'

'No. You?'

'Uh-uh.'

We contemplate this absence. I am trying to remember

what I was like when I was sixteen. What was it I saw in Annie? Oh, yes. That. No doubt my girlfriend is trying to remember what it was like when she first fell for a boy.

'It's all happening too fast for me,' I say.

'Well, get used to it.'

'She told me he's not special.'

'She told me he is.'

'And you believe it?'

'Well, he's coming to meet us.'

'So it must be serious.'

This requires some thought. Boy as in *boy*. Boy as in stage three of the parenting adventure. Nappies, schools and boys. Done the nappies, got my head around Key Stage Four maths (harder than it looks) and now we have the boy. Boy as in the gathering of rosebuds, as in time's wing'd chariot, as in someone to make brooches and toys for her delight. That sort of boy. Boy as in the sudden blossoming of desire. Boy who – for heaven's sake – she thinks might be the one. Just like she thinks my girlfriend is the one. Boy as in the speaker in Andrew Marvell's paean to lust:

> *Let us roll all our strength, and all*
> *Our sweetness, up into one ball...*

Yes, well, we'll see about that. Some of us had to mislearn the names of the stars, you know, before we got round to rolling our strength (and all our sweetness) up into one ball. And even then we ended up looking at whisky-stained mug shots of Don Bradman. But I turned out alright, didn't I? Waiting like the good Catholic boy I never quite was never did me any harm. These are battles – is that the word? – to come. For the moment our daughter has a boy and the pair of them are 'going out', whatever that means, and have been, in secret, for an eternity of three weeks. And now he is coming to visit. And I am please to behave myself.

'When is he coming?' I ask.

'Today.'

'Today when?'

'Later.'

I was hoping for something more specific, but it is in the nature of these things that the comings and goings of teenagers cannot be specified by conventional means or without at least four phone calls and seven supplementaries. The supplementaries may be texts, e-mails or instant messages. It doesn't much matter. He will get here when he gets here.

London, 1992

I have a confession. I keep a diary of sorts. A collection of jottings. Ramblings and curiosities. Snatches of conversation. Images that stick. Notes on names. A reminder of 'what it was to be me', according to Joan Didion. She wrote a celebrated essay on 'why I keep a diary' once. Perhaps she is right. I don't know. I've always done it and I guess it's partly from habit and partly from need. Unstructured, undisciplined and discursive. When my daughter was born I stopped for a while. After all, we were busy. The whole parenting adventure swept over us like a wave on a sunlit beach. A revolution in our lives. One minute we were basking in the young dual-income professional sun. The next we were body-surfing the waves of an unpredictable ocean of negative equity, nappies and nursery fees. Tumbling and turning in the foaming water.

Cresting the exhilarating wave and then crashing with it, hoping there were no rocks and delighted only to find ourselves bumping against the sandy bottom. Tumbling some more and struggling for breath before we emerged, breathless and grinning, onto the unfamiliar shore. We gulped in air, looked at each other and said, 'Let's do it again.' My New Year's resolution, back when I still made them, back when I thought I was in control of my life, was to bring a little bit of order to my jottings. This was 1 January 1992. The way I saw it the most important thing in my life was my daughter and I resolved to write her a letter every day. That would be my diary. Notes on a life we'd made. Notes on a life we *would* make. There was an old man, a friend of a friend, with grey eyes and smile lines.

'A daughter?' he asked.

I nodded.

'You're a lucky man...'

It felt that way.

'... because you're about to experience the greatest love you'll ever know.'

Of course I missed writing anything on the first day. I never was much good at resolutions. And, having missed it, I have no memory of what we did that day. January 1 1992? Perhaps nothing. Perhaps I just stared at the television and watched the Soviet Union disappear into nothingness. Its too, too sullied flesh seemed by some unspecified alchemy to thaw and resolve itself into a dew. 'What happens to your fist when you open your hand?' I wrote the next day. 'Does it disappear? Did it never exist?' The sort of nonsense I write when I've been brooding too long or eating too much. But we must have been in London because that's where we were the following day, on 2 January. According to the letter I wrote in my daughter's diary, we went for a walk in the nearby park, where she watched the ants in the grass with a consuming curiosity. Literally. She was choosing which one to eat, but that turned out not to be such a great idea. The ants resisted and she tried to spit them out in disgust. Only they wouldn't come, so she did a kind of reverse lick to smear the ants onto her hand before holding it up triumphantly for me to see.

She wasn't quite walking then. She was at the stand-and-flap stage. She would get upright and use her arms to keep her balance without ever quite managing to take a step. As her balance became more precarious she would flap her arms faster and faster, like a bird learning to fly. You see them on nature programmes, teetering on the edge of the nest, flapping desperately. Sometimes they fall. Sometimes they fly. And sometimes they swim. The German poet Rainer Maria Rilke wrote a poem that sticks in my mind. It was about a swan. The bird, so ungainly on land, 'labouring through what is still undone', is transformed by water. So clumsy on land, so regal on the glassy surface of the floating stream. Probably Rilke was talking about the move from life to death. Death, he's suggesting, may be our better milieu. I don't believe a word of it. Life's for living. You just have to know how to fly.

London, 2007

'Any sign of him?' I ask.

My girlfriend shakes her head. I roll my eyes. She gives me a look. My son and I dump our cricket stuff in the hallway and I go up to shower. We've just been in the nets for an hour. Which is to say he's been in the nets and I've been bowling to him. Something new for me. I always hated bowling. Hated that smug look batsmen get when they hit you (not the ball, you) over your head for four or six. It is a curiosity of cricket terminology that a batsman seldom hits the ball for six. Cricket is much more personal than that. He hits the bowler for six. He may 'punish the bowling' but when he hits something, it's always the bowler. And I always hated that. Hated making so much effort for so little reward. Hedgehog and foxes, you see, in Isaiah Berlin's celebrated formulation. He was writing about Tolstoy, but the idea works for cricket. It starts with something the Greek poet Archilochus wrote: 'The fox knows many things, but the hedgehog knows one big thing.' Berlin takes this idea and expands it to describe two kinds of writers – those who see the world through a single defining idea (Hegel, Nietzsche) and those who see the world as complex, contradictory and, well, more interesting than that (Shakespeare, Joyce). Bowlers are the hedgehogs who know one big thing. Batsmen are the foxes who know many small things.

But one consequence of having a son to bowl at is my bowling has got a lot better. I can hit a line and a length. I can even get the ball to move a little. I resolve not to let anyone know. The last thing I want is for people to start thinking of me as a bowler.

'I'll go and shower then.'

'You might want to shave as well,' says my girlfriend.

'Why?'

'Well, you know. It makes you look…' Her eyes start to flicker, which is what they do when she knows she's on dodgy ground. '…younger.'

'Nice save.' I've got to give her that.

'Thanks.'

I go upstairs to shower (and shave). As I lather up I look at myself in the mirror. It's going to take some work to make me look younger, what with the head like the Millennium Dome (only without the yellow pointy bits) and the white hair curling around my ears. Maybe my girlfriend is right. Maybe I should keep it short. Maybe if I get rid of a few nose hairs. Maybe...

I shave carefully. I look at least a week younger. Younger than I looked, not younger than I am. In that sense I have always been old.

I am in the bedroom when (in his own sweet time) my daughter's boy arrives. I can hear him being introduced to my girlfriend downstairs. He's not from London. I can't be much more specific than that. I'm not very good at accents. He has the flat vowels and curiously downbeat tones of, well, north of Watford. I listen a bit more carefully. Not Yorkshire and not Brum. Okay, so that narrows it down a bit. I can define him by what he is not. Not Liverpool. Not Newcastle. Not Scotland or Ireland. Not Wales. Not the West Country. What does that leave us? East Midlands, I would guess. Nottingham? Leicester? Something like that. Nottingham sounds alright, although I've never been to Trent Bridge...

I would go down and say hello but the fact of the matter is that I have got myself into something of a pickle. It is a Saturday and I am listening to Sports Roundup on the BBC World Service. They're talking about the forthcoming Cricket World Cup in the West Indies. I am not a big fan of the one-day game, but, well, cricket is cricket. Prompted by the discussion on the radio I have been reliving – is that the word? – Kevin Pietersen's outrageous reverse sweep from the previous year when he hit Muralitharan, the Sri Lankan bowler, for six at Edgbaston. Hit the bowler, not the ball, remember. I imagine Murali, his permanent, gleaming smile sparkling like the Indian Ocean, doing cartwheels as he spins away over backward point and lands, right side up, between a hamper from Fortnum & Mason and a burly Aussie piloting twelve pints through the crowd. Pietersen's shot was truly remarkable – remarkable because it was premeditated, remarkable because it was stupid, remarkable because it worked. And remarkable because he hit the damn thing so hard. 'Well, well,' said the commentator on television. 'Whatever next?' A good question. With Pietersen you hardly know what next. You count yourself lucky if you know what just happened.

I can't imagine how he hit that reverse sweep for six. He says he practises it, for heaven's sake. At nets at the club we all tried it. Some of the younger ones, the guys with good eyes and fast feet, manage to get in position. But can they hit it? Maybe, by fluke. Mostly they trip and fall. Rob turns up his nose.

'I don't see why you would want to do it,' he says. 'I mean, where's the percentage?' The percentage is an elusive grail sought by batsmen in a pickle. I have to admit, there is no percentage in it. But still, I am interested in how he manages it. Does he do it for hours in the nets? He takes guard? As the bowler takes his delivery stride, Pietersen leaps like a startled frog to stand the other way? He changes hands? And he clips the ball over mid-wicket? Even without an audience, it just doesn't make sense. You can't generate the power. You can't keep your balance. You can't get the timing right.

So bear with me for a moment while I confess that in the privacy of my bedroom I have tried to recreate the shot. And in the process I have done what he should have done – but didn't. What Pietersen did was walk down the pitch as though nothing had happened and start gesticulating at the people obscuring the Pavilion side screen. In 2008 he did the same thing to the New Zealand bowler, Scott Styris. Reverse swept him for six over what would have been extra cover but which had become mid-wicket by the time Pietersen had turned himself into a left-hander. 'Like watching Gilchrist pull,' said the commentator on *TMS* and for all the listeners this would have been enough to understand what had happened. Adam Gilchrist, the Australian wicket keeper, has one of the most astonishingly aggressive pull shots in the game. He doesn't so much go 'back and across' as 'forward and across'. And here Pietersen was matching it. It brought to mind Ginger Rogers's comment on her dancing with Fred Astaire. She did everything he did 'backwards and in heels'. Well, Pietersen doesn't have the heels, but he did do it backwards. And later in the match he didn't so much reverse sweep as reverse drive Styris over what had become wide mid-on. Except it was mid-off when Styris started to bowl. 'No one,' said Jonathan Agnew, 'has ever hit a shot like that.' The crowd, according to the BBC website, were 'bug-eyed with delight' and even Styris had to laugh.

What I have done, by contrast, is all too predictable. I have lost my balance. I have stumbled and fallen over. I have cracked my head on the shelf next to my bed and one lens of my glasses has bounced out and gone somewhere behind and beneath the bed.

Which is where I am. Half naked. And not even the respectable half.

'Mum,' says my daughter. 'Where's Dad?'

'Upstairs, I guess.'

'Okay.'

I hear footsteps on the landing. My daughter is giving her boy a tour of the house. 'There's the bathroom,' she says. 'Sorry about the glass door. If you want to shower, we can make sure no one comes near.'

What does she mean 'shower'? Is he planning to spend the night?

'And this is my parents' bedroom.' There are sounds of shuffling as they peer around the door. It is dusk and the room is quite dark. Only my feet are showing from beneath the bed. I hold my breath.

'What's with the radio?' says the young man.

'Oh, don't worry about that,' says my daughter. 'Cricket, I guess. Dad wouldn't be Dad without cricket on the radio.'

'Really? That's, like, so *old*.'

'You'll see. He's going to talk to you about cricket.'

'Why?'

'I don't know. I mean, I guess it's just what he does.'

'But I don't know nothing about cricket.'

'Yeah, well, don't worry about it.'

'What will I say?'

'I don't know. Just smile and nod. That's what I do.'

'Really?'

'Yeah. And tell him how young he looks. He likes that.'

I LOVE …

Making radio contact

The trouble with losing your glasses when you're myopic is you can't see to find the damn things. But after a few minutes' groping I clasp the lens and emerge from beneath the bed. It's a nice bed. There's a duvet with a bright red cover. My girlfriend bought it at one of those places where they offer to wrap things for you on the presumption that no one would spend that much money on themselves. It has to be a gift for someone else. My girlfriend claims she got it 'for a song' but I know better than to believe her. She only says it to pander to my puritan sensibilities. She worries that I think she spends too much on luxuries. She secretly thinks I would be as happy living in a pigsty as I am in our home in north London. There are times when I think she's right. I would be just as happy anywhere. You know the kind of thing. A loaf of bread, a glass of wine and thou. What else do you need? Apart from a bat and ball, of course.

London, 1993

My girlfriend is pregnant for the second time. I am clearly in some sort of introspective mood. In my daughter's diary I write lists of what I want for her: 'confidence, curiosity, courage, love and laughter'. I am 'very aware how closely you imitate us', how our little mannerisms, our every gesture, our patterns of speech, our tempers and our smiles get played back to us. She has her own room, but recently she has started coming through to climb into bed with us. 'It's not much fun,' I wrote as lovingly as I could. 'You keep kicking me where no man deserves to be kicked.' She is an uncomfortable bedfellow. If she's asleep she wriggles and kicks, gurgles and snorts. If she's awake she blows raspberries on my back or drips water from her bottle into my ear. We recently bought an extra large bed to cope with this. It stretches out for two metres and more in every direction. A huge bed. A wonderful bed. A bed you can lose yourself in. And still she finds us, and gurgles happily and kicks me in the groin. For us it is a bed of memories. All our lives have been lived there and all our dreams.

Fifteen years later we still have the same bed. Today three of the four pillows have the same slips as the duvet. They are also warm and soft and red and welcoming. The fourth is a sort of mottled beige. It may once have been yellow. There are diagrams of animals drawn – or pretending to have been drawn – in a child's hand. The animals are labelled alphabetically. Aardvark. Bear. Cheetah. Dog. The cotton is beginning to fray. There are almost bare patches where the pillow shows through. The mattress is thick and soft and comfortable. We've had it for a couple of years now. Maybe three. Four even. It's also beginning to show its age, even though we turn it regularly. Or maybe it is beginning to show our age. It is a bed for old people. For a couple who have been together longer than they remember. There are two slight-but-notice-able hollows, one for me and one for my girlfriend. Hers is on the right, next to her dresser, the window, the mirror and the impala pelt she bought in a moment of – well, I would say weakness; she would say nothing. The moment does not need qualification – so we'll just say 'next to the impala skin'. My side is on the right, next to a pile of sweaty sports shoes. Hockey shoes, tennis shoes, running shoes, cricket shoes. They also need no qualification.

And the radio. It is the radio that brings you to my bed at all. I wouldn't have mentioned it but for the radio. They're previewing the coming Cricket World Cup and in the process are reviewing the winter tour to Australia. The line being put out is that the Australia tour was a mixed bag. We were hammered in the Ashes, but did well in the one-dayers. It was a mixed bag but not an unmitigated disaster. This is nonsense. The disaster was entirely without mitigation. Games that should have been won (Adelaide) were lost. Balls that should have landed on the pitch (Harmison) landed on the moon. The one-day series was without any consequence (you have only to look at England's subsequent performance in the Cricket World Cup to know that). What mattered were the Ashes – and the Ashes were lost. And it was such a let-down, following the wonderful, exhilarating, belief-beggaring, Ashes series of the summer of 2005 when England won the series and our hearts, when Freddie Flintoff revealed he was both superhuman and a super human and when Kevin Pietersen showed himself to be more than a swaggering small-town boy from, well, my home town.

Every innings is a story and no two innings are the same. You have only to read the cricket reports in the national press. Each has a natural 'arc' – a beginning, a middle and an end.

Even one that lasts only one ball. Every human frailty is there.

Summer. A wet match on a wet pitch. Rob wins the toss and puts our hosts in to bat. Brave or foolish, only time will tell. The pitch has a steep slope that makes it difficult for batsmen. Rob's looking for slip catches. No doubt he has read reports in the *New Scientist* that the crocodiles of Kruger National Park are dying off in their hundreds. Scientists are unsure why, but it appears to be to do with unnaturally hardened fatty deposits in their tails. Some say it is their diet; others say it is something in the water. In any case there have been photographs of rows of vast, scaly-backed, malevolent, pot-bellied creatures, looking hungry and dangerous, and who can doubt that this is on the skipper's mind as he sets a slip cordon of me, Woolfie, Spibes and Joe to the bowling of the Prince and the Spaniard? But it was Shiv-the-blade who came on first change and did the damage. Bowling up the hill and into the wind, he ran through the opposition card. It was great cricket. Unable to score – there was a purple patch just before drinks when the Spaniard and Shiv bowled seven consecutive maidens – the hosts resorted to foolish shots. At one stage they were 60 for eight and they are all out for 98. We look forward to tea knowing we need only 99 to win.

'I don't like this,' says Rob. 'I'd rather chase 200.'

'Not an easy pitch,' I agree.

But also not an easy total. Batsmen don't know how to behave. Do they try to make it quickly? Or do they settle in for a patient 30 overs?

Only 99 runs. Joe and Woolfie strode out to the pitch like men without a care in the world. I settled down with a crossword. Pete lit up and closed his eyes to the sun. Andy smiled at strangers. Even Rob, briefly, looked relaxed, a feat he has not achieved since that time when... well, never mind. But the fact is it was not easy. The pitch was still slow. The field was vast and the boundary a long way off. The bowling was straight. The fielders were sharp and chirpy... and wickets fell. First Joe, then Woolfie. Then Rob and Andy. Everyone gets in. Everyone gets out. Still, at 55 for four, with Spibes and me at the crease, the match looks safe enough... but then Spibes was out LBW and suddenly the 44 runs needed for victory seemed a long way off. Especially when Pete fell cheaply.

But with the Spaniard and me, Balfour, at the crease, all would be well. Surely?

We took it carefully. In an unprecedented display of discipline and good sense, I block seven balls in a row before the opposition leggie bowls a loose one and I can open my shoulders and dispatch it into the greenhouses beyond the trees. An audible sigh runs round the ground, but quickly the tension sets in again. We are within six runs of victory when I'm beaten by a ball that holds up slightly. I drove, it popped up, and I was out, caught at mid-on for twenty-something.

In comes Jack. Five needed. Three wickets in hand. Out goes Jack Lancaster. In comes Shiv. The Spaniard, going for glory, pulls a full toss, but his timing is off and he top edges it into the skies. Three needed. Nine wickets down. In strides the Prince.

At this point, dear readers, I must ask those of a delicate sensibility to look away, for I must describe the scenes on the terraces and it does not make for pretty reading. First there was our skipper. A man whose whole life was flashing before his eyes, in an ever-accelerating vortex of doom. Not normally a religious man (in fact, not normal at all), he can be heard reciting the Kyrie Eleison to himself, first in Greek and then in Latin. Could he ever show his face at the club again if the third eleven team he captains lost chasing 99? He would have to leave the club. Leave London. Leave the country. He would join the Foreign Legion. Become a monk. Have a sex change. Anything would be better than this. And Andy? Andy has given up rolling fags and gone straight for eating the tobacco. He doesn't even bother to chew. Pete can't bear the tension and goes to put his head in a bucket of cold water. And Jack has developed a consuming interest in his ankles, like a man searching his ankles for nits.

But we reckon without Shiv-the-knife. A man who has bowled his side to easy victory (assuming his teammates could bat) is not about to let it slip away. He blocks and blocks again and soon enough a wide, a no ball and a bye see us to what, from the myopic comfort of the bar, we will later describe as an 'easy victory by one wicket'.

I emerge triumphant from beneath the bed, clean up, replace the missing lens in my glasses and go downstairs. There is no sign of my daughter, the big one, or her young man. They have disappeared into the forbidden city of her bedroom.

'Well,' I say to my girlfriend. 'What do we think?'

She gives me a warning look.

'We think he's lovely,' she says pointedly. She doesn't mean he is lovely. She isn't expressing a view on the young man at all. What she means is I must behave myself. What she means is this is something new in our lives and she expects me, against all the odds, and in defiance of every precedent during the past decade and a half, to rise to the challenge. She expects me to be better than I am. She expects me to be warm and welcoming and, well, mature. She expects me to allow our daughter the space and the time and the support to explore her accession to adulthood. She expects me, in short, to shut up.

Her eyes move to a point in the middle distance, somewhere beyond my right shoulder. There is the sound of shuffling shoes, of hands buried in pockets, of low-slung jeans dragging on polished floors. There is the smell of industrial volumes of Lynx. Although, by the way, I have no doubt that were a lynx to smell it, it would run a mile.

'Dad,' says my daughter. 'This is...'

'Hello,' I say. 'Pleased to meet you.'

'Yeah, alright?' he replies.

I LOVE …

Marking the boundary

We shall get back to that 'Yeah, alright' in a minute. By my reckoning it falls some distance short of the 'Good evening, how are you? Pleased to meet you, sir' school of manners I deployed with such limited effect in conversation with people like Annie's father. It compares unfavourably with the line of young suitors, some of them wearing ties, who would come to our door in search of my sister but who would first pay homage to my parents by making – enduring – polite conversation with my father about molecular biology or the price of tea in China or whatever other subject he chose for their torment that day. No Lacanian analysis required to deconstruct those conversations: 'So you're planning to study law?' says my father, meaning, 'You've got more chance of making partner in your first year of articles than you have of getting into my daughter's trousers, got that, sonny?' By the same token there was no need to have read widely to understand my sister's 'Da-ad?' Meaning:

1. I decide who gets into my trousers and
2. Frankly I agree about this one, but then again
3. He does have a car and

4. There is a party at the beach tonight and since you won't let me drive (and yes I know I don't have a licence yet) what's a girl to do and
5. Anyway, he's not that bad. You should see some of the others.

But for the moment I have more pressing things to think about. The first, and most obvious, is that my daughter, the beautiful, incomparably lovely fulfilment of my dreams, the bundle of joy who poked her sleepy nose into the world nearly sixteen years ago, looks surprisingly like, well, a woman. A person who makes her own decisions. A fully fledged (Is that the word? Do children fledge? And does that explain the smell coming from my son's bedroom? He is twelve and his body is going through what the school textbooks used to describe as a 'period of rapid change', which he cunningly disguises by spraying something which the advertisements say will make him irresistible to girls but which to me smells suspiciously like industrial effluent under his armpits and, for all I know, in other nooks and crannies as well) young woman with recently cut and styled hair, intelligent eyes and a nervous smile.

The smile is her version of my girlfriend's look. It says I am please to behave myself. I am please not to say anything stupid or clever. Which, by the way, leaves me with little option. 'Stupid' and 'clever' are my default positions in conversations with my children. You would have thought this left a broad area in the middle for potential consensus, but in fact it does not because 'clever' and 'stupid' are in fact the same thing. It is merely a question of interpretation. What I regard as clever, witty, urbane, charming and challenging tends to be classified simply as 'stupid'. What I regard as mundane, run-of-the-mill and obvious is sometimes accredited as 'clever'.

Furthermore I am (please) not to ask awkward questions. I am not to talk about politics, race, class, economics, literature, theatre or music that doesn't involve someone who sounds like he or she is in great pain and in need of medication. I should under no circumstances mention crosswords, bridge or the world price of cocoa. I am (please) to make every effort to appear normal, and if at all possible I am to say nothing at all.

Alright?

Well, no, but let's take it one step at a time, shall we?

At our club the boundary marker is half hosepipe, half rope. The hosepipe is a bit of a problem, actually. It is attached to a tap in the corner near the tennis courts and the year-long drip tends to create something of a quagmire just in the path where people have to squeeze between the courts and the score box to get to the other side where the nets are. Mind you, the rope's not much better. It is too thin and tends to get lost from sight the minute the grass grows a little. Over the years it has taken on the colour of the earth and mulch. In autumn it gets buried under the leaves and acorns that fall from the line of oaks along the northern end of the field. I prefer the fields where they mark the boundary in white chalk, with little flags every now and then to assist the umpires. There's one like that at the corner of Hampstead Heath, near where we live. Before the game starts you can walk the line, putting out flags every twenty paces or so. It's a pleasant ritual, a time to contemplate the game to come, to assess the weather and the wind, to note the longish grass in the outfield. 'Going to have to work for our runs,' you say to yourself. 'No easy boundaries today.' And halfway round you stop for a moment to imagine the six you're going to hit over long on, the one that clears the boundary and then some. The one that carries the ball into the crowd. Or that clears the line and the crowd and the very stadium itself. Like that time at the Oval in the 2007 one-day series against the West Indies when Morton carved Sidebottom over mid-wicket so high and hard and far that the ball landed in the road beyond. You know the one.

It's the six you've never hit.

London 1993

Of course I record cricket scores as well. They're there jotted in the margin. 'Today we went for a walk in the park. You tried to eat an acorn and hurt your gum. I bought you a lolly to take away the pain.' And in the corner. 'England 106-2.' No note of whom England were playing or where or when. Just a mention of a score, presumably at close of play, that once must have meant something to me. And sometimes there is more detail. On 23 August 1993 England won a consolation victory over Australia at the Oval. It didn't much matter. Australia had won that Ashes series long before they got to Kennington (the final result was 4-1 in their favour). But it was nice to listen to. Most of the English batsmen got a few runs. Gooch made half centuries in both innings. But most important, of course, the bowlers did what you have to do to win a Test match: you have to bowl the opposition out twice. Always difficult at the Oval, which is known as a batsman's pitch. Angus Fraser, a man of whom it was once said that you could tell he would never tell a lie just from watching him bowl, plugged away on line and length, and ended up with match figures of eight for one hundred and something.

On 23 August 1993 I shouldn't have been paying attention to the cricket. I was in the delivery room of the hospital in east London, watching our second child being born. Wondering if some clown was kicking in our car window. Again the labour was long and hard, but it was not as long or as hard. And it happened during office hours. None of this strength-sapping through-the-night nonsense of the first time. I say office hours; what I mean is 'cricket hours'. I could – and did – get regular updates on events at the Oval from a Trinidadian nurse. Every so often she popped her head round the door to report that another Australian wicket had fallen. One hundred and six for six. One hundred and forty-two for seven. For a while it looked as if the Australians might hold out, but eventually the last wicket fell with the score on 229. They were chasing 391 to win. An impossible target. They lost, we won – all was well with the world. And – just before the six o'clock news – our second daughter was born.

'She's my little sister,' our elder daughter told everyone for weeks after that. 'She's the little one and I'm the big one.'

One happy effect of the arrival of the new child was that for a few months our elder daughter became mine completely. My girlfriend was busy. She had our younger daughter to contend with. Our elder daughter and I found refuge in the second bedroom. It was there we could sleep in peace. It was there we made a den beneath the bunk bed and shot bears with our fingers. It was there we invented the story game. The story game is simple. She chooses 'a thing' – which may be an event or a character or a colour. Then she holds out her thumb. I suck it and – as if by magic! – a story appears incorporating the thing she has selected. We draw heavily on our experiences in South Africa. My brother works in one of the premier game reserves and we have seen for ourselves the great grey mounds of rhino middens and the rampaging effects of hungry elephants. Although in truth she prefers the gentler stories. She is not that interested in my versions of the Elephant's Child and its insatiable curiosity. She does not much mind how a rhino marks its turf. She has seen rhinos and she knows that all they do is stand around all day. Some nights I am tired and the stories are no good. And some nights I am on form and the stories appear perfectly formed. 'This evening,' I wrote in 1995, 'it was a "pie contest, a tortoise and a giraffe".' I – or rather, her thumb – came up with a story that involved a tortoise pretending to be a pie. 'At the end your only comment was that the story "didn't have enough giraffe" and you went to sleep on the understanding that I'll tell the story again, but with more giraffe.' She is an appreciative audience. She claps her hands and laughs. She lies on her back and kicks her feet in the air. I notice patterns and tailor the stories to suit her. She likes sad middles and happy endings. She likes danger, but not to 'her thing' or 'her' – for often she chooses to be the hero. She prefers homecomings to departures. She likes her food.

'What will be in the story tonight?' I ask.

She pretends to think.

'A little big girl with blonde hair like mine,' she says. 'And an ice cream.'

And you can bet that no matter how grubby her thumb, or how long I suck it, or what wild animals intervene, a story will emerge about a little big girl with blonde hair who gets an ice cream in the final scene.

London 2007

They bring the boundary in for Twenty20. To make the game more exciting, they say, by which they mean 'to make it easier for the batsmen to hit sixes'. But in other games they make the field as big as possible. My club ground is not very big. Wider than it is long. The easiest scoring shot is the lofted straight drive. Bang it back over the bowler's head and you've a good chance of hitting a six. When we mark out the field we push the boundary as deep as possible. The fielders at mid-off and mid-on (or fine leg and third man) are standing right up against the oak trees that line that end of the field. On practice nights we take turns to stand in their deep shade while someone hits towering catches in our direction. The interplay of shadow and light, the confused background, the swirling wind, the acorns on the ground... they all conspire to make those catches even more difficult than they would be. But we don't mind. It's all part of the game. The point is that for the longer game it is better to have the field as big as possible.

But who knows if we're in this for the long haul?

He looks just like any other kid of his generation. He has long hair and a thin face, impossibly slim hips and a soft, darting smile. He is wearing a T-shirt and a 'hoodie' although the hood is not up, but lies in soft furls around his surprisingly thin neck. Not that it matters. His hair is hoodie enough. No cop looking at grainy CCTV pictures would be able to identify him behind all that hair. It hangs down below his shoulders in a tumult of waves and curls. It hangs down over his eyes too and from time to time he flicks his head to clear it, albeit momentarily, from his eyes. It is parted, more or less, to one side and the recurrent flicking and the parting mean that his head hangs a little to one side. Or perhaps this is just because he is tall. Taller than me, in fact. It is a while since anyone looked down at me. Not that I don't know what it's like. My father was taller than me and my brother outstrips me by a couple of inches. But here, in my own house, I am without question the daddy. No one else can reach the microwave, which we forgot to include when redesigning the kitchen and which now is three feet higher than it should be. No one else (although give my son a few more months) can find the chocolates I have hidden on the top shelf. And now here's this young man looking down his nose at me. I guess I'm going to have to get used to it. He has big brown eyes and delicate, long fingers. His nails are neatly trimmed. He scores pretty well in the 'first glance' assessment I give him. The fringe is a problem, but perhaps he can be encouraged to cut his hair. With the wisdom of hindsight I can tell you that, actually, he is rather good-looking, but that's because I have seen him suntanned by the lake in France where we went in the summer. Unconventionally handsome, people would say. Nothing is quite in proportion, but everything works. But back then? Back then I saw a shuffling, gawky teenager wondering whether my daughter was worth it.

The 'it', you understand, being me.

His clothes are neat, though, and clean. He wears jeans and sneakers. He dresses, in fact, just like my daughter. Except that he is a lot taller than her, they could share clothes. They have that curious, androgynous style popular with a certain kind of urban kid. There are borderline hints of goth. The skull on the T-shirt, the slogan on the hoodie. The silver bracelet. But they are only hints. His primary loyalty is to skateboarding and therefore to the soft clothing favoured by those who rip up our pavements on their boards. I know this about him. It is his passion. It's how they met.

It was at a skate park in Camden in London. She was hanging out with her friends, hoping to meet boys. He was skating with his mates and hoping, I have no doubt, to be met by girls. There is no diary entry to record these events. By the time my daughter was thirteen or fourteen, I had stopped writing her diary. It was time for her to have her own memories – that was my excuse anyway. It's not that I stopped making notes. It's just that I stopped writing to her. In hindsight, of course, I know why I stopped. Puberty. She had become a woman and this was necessarily private from me. I had been a child. I understood what that was about. But I had never been a young woman and, mostly, I didn't have a clue what she was going through. And so to make notes on what she was up to was – what's the word? – unseemly. Intrusive. Pretentious. Presumptuous.

Well, all of those – but mostly it was uncomfortable. So I let her diary slide. By then I had other children to whom I could write. For a while her diary stood on a shelf in the living room. Then one day it got tidied away into my study. But I spend far too much money buying books I will never get round to reading and every so often it becomes necessary to do a cull of the shelves. The diary went back downstairs. To the cellar this time, where it joined some old photographs and some balls of wool bought inexplicably on a trip to Crete many years before. I have memories, though, and I have other records. My letters to friends are dotted with references to the boy wonder. You can hear my tone. It is deliberately neutral. I have taken my girlfriend's looks to heart. I am saying nothing…

After the skate park, the ensuing courtship took place on

MSN and via text. He came down a few more times to skate. They hung out some more. Glances were exchanged. Hands accidentally brushed each other as they sat under the shade of an oak tree. At some point there must have been a fumbling kiss. Who knows, perhaps the fumbling went further than that? Ours is not to inquire. Personally I suspect the oak tree played a part. There is a particular oak favoured by teenagers. Its branches hang down and lightly graze the ground. One year they cut it back, and exposed for all the world the flattened grass beneath. But it had grown out again. And inside, inside is a safe, warm, dry bower, free from the prying eyes of passing parents. You can stand in there, hidden from the passing throng. You can kiss, and no one but you would know. And so all we know is that after some weeks my daughter made her announcement. 'It' was official. He would like to meet us. And, oh, by the way, could he 'stay at ours' for the night?

He could. He did. He slept on the sofa. He had lots of hair and spoke with what I had by now discovered was definitely an East Midlands accent. He said 'thank you' and 'no thank you' and not much else. And sometimes not even that.

'I've got to say something?' I had said earlier. 'There must be something we can talk about.'

My daughter screwed up her nose. It's what she does when she's making unpleasant choices.

'If you must,' she said, 'you can talk about sport.'

Only I didn't hear the 'sport' part. What I heard was 'cricket'.

Which made everything alright. Because if we had cricket in common the rest would be easy. Cricket would be the great lubricant. Cricket would be the cement that binds. Cricket, the sport made for poetry, would be the balm, the oil on troubled waters, the sugar frosting on the cake of this new-found friendship. He hadn't chosen me and I definitely hadn't chosen him, but everything was possible because we had cricket in common.

Except we didn't.

I LOVE ...

Other men's flowers

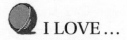

Has she warned him about me? I suppose she must have. A thoughtful girl, our daughter. A strategist. Understands why you might hold up your ace for a round or two in bridge. She knows how to lose one trick now to save two later. What advice did she give him, apart from 'smile and nod'? To talk about cricket (sorry, Annie) or not to talk about cricket? On the evidence you would say her advice has been that he should not talk at all. About cricket or anything else. Dinner is over and the two of them are itching to leave the table. We don't live on a sugar farm south of Durban. We live in a terraced house in north London. Our garden is slightly smaller than our living room. There is no stretch of lawn leading down to a swing by the sugar fields. There are no bush pigs rustling in the cane. There are no dogs barking to the moon. I mean, there are dogs – how else do you explain the state of our pavements every morning – but they are indoors, watching TV like their owners. There are not even any stars to look at. We live in the city and the city means light. A soft orange glow is as dark as it ever gets. Even without cloud cover, the stars are barely visible. Sometimes, one day in 50, you get a cold clear night and, if you're in a darker than usual spot, you might be lucky and see Venus rising. But mostly? Mostly there are no stars at all. Mostly our version of the heavens is the glow of the street lamps and our rustling cane is the swish of car tyres on tar.

Except for Hampstead Heath. Hampstead Heath is our wilderness. Officially it belongs to the Corporation of London, but I think of it as mine. I have walked its every path and catalogued its benches. I know it in summer and winter, by day and by night. I have sat on it and listened to the city go to sleep and I have walked it just as the city rises. They say that London's parks are 'gardens for the gardenless' and the Heath is mine. Seven or eight hundred acres of paths and grass, of hill and dale on our doorstep. Mind you, I suspect most of the people in our part of north London think of it the same way. Certainly their children do. It's where teenagers gather as darkness falls.

'Thanks for dinner, Dad,' says our daughter.

'You're welcome.'

'Thank you,' says her boy.

He is also welcome. To all three helpings. Which disappeared without a trace, the way a Michael Vaughan pull shot speeds past mid-wicket for four. Watch Vaughan do it sometime. In cricket the batsman has less than half a second to react. The decision to pull is instantaneous and irrevocable. Vaughan is a delight to watch. There are some batsmen you sense play the pull shot with their eyes closed. Not Vaughan. He sees it all the way. In his comeback Test at Headingley in 2007, the first he had played after a long lay-off from injury, he made a gritty hundred. His elation was palpable; the delight of his home crowd infectious. Buoyed by this he pulled the next ball off Taylor. Sweetly crisply, perfectly... down Morton's throat. For a moment no one noticed. Vaughan had hit the ball so perfectly that everyone thought it had gone for six. It was only when they looked a second time that the commentators realised that Morton had taken the catch inches in from the boundary rope.

I suppose it is because the boy doesn't talk that he can eat so much so fast. But I am mindful of my girlfriend's looks and I say nothing about the equation that every father knows by heart where their daughters and their boyfriends are concerned: boy + food = energy = ?

'Um,' says our daughter. 'We're just going for a walk on the Heath.'

'Okay,' says my girlfriend. Before I can get a word in. And before I offer any sage advice. You can't blame the kids for wanting to go out. It's been a wet spring, but tonight is lovely. A perfect evening with plenty of warmth in the sky and late blossom on the trees.

'Have fun,' says my girlfriend. What is she thinking about? What happened to 'Don't do anything I wouldn't do'?

'Bye,' I call. The door slams. In time I will come to recognise it as the sound of summer. A 'bye' swallowed by a slamming door as they head for the Heath. From time to time in England you will meet people for whom John Arlott was the 'sound of summer'. For three decades and more he commentated on the cricket for the BBC. His last broadcast was in 1980. Too late for me. I arrived in Britain in 1984 and I never heard Arlott 'live'. It was before my time. I have since, in documentaries on the BBC. It's a gravelly, gorgeous, confident voice. I have read since of his wonderful gift for a turn of phrase – he once described Clive Lloyd pulling a ball into the Mound Stand at Lord's as 'the stroke of a man knocking a thistle top off with a walking stick'. He was commentating for the BBC when Donald Bradman was out for his duck at the Oval in 1948. Even to read his words now sends a shiver down my spine. What it must have been to hear them.

> *Hollies pitches the ball up slowly and... he's bowled... Bradman bowled Hollies nought... bowled Hollies nought... and what do you say under these circumstances?*

What indeed? Fortunately Arlott was the artist for the occasion and he knew what to say.

> *I wonder if you see the ball very clearly in your last Test in England, on a ground where you've played some of the biggest cricket in your life and where the opposing side has just stood round you and given you three cheers and the crowd has clapped you all the way to the wicket. I wonder if you see the ball at all.*

I don't see how you possibly can. I choke up just reading it, for heaven's sake. There's a lump in my throat and my eyes are moist. I don't see how Bradman could have seen a damn thing. But then maybe he was tougher than me. A sideline for Arlott was his poetry. He wrote some. *The MCC Anthology of Cricket Verse* has four of his poems, but he was perhaps better known for the readings he made of other men's works. Louis MacNeice, the cricketing humanist, was a favourite, as was Dylan Thomas. For all that I never heard him, when I hear people describe Arlott's commentaries, when I see the faraway look in their eyes, I feel I am in good company. I understand the intimacy of a good radio voice. I have been in love with the radio since a very early age. Whisper it, but it's true. I was nine years old when my grandmother died and my first thought was, I hope I get the radio. My parents had bought it for her for her birthday only a few months earlier. It was a 'transistor radio', which is to say it was black and shiny, had a leather cover and worked the moment you turned it on, unlike the old valve radio in the corner of the sitting room which took an age to warm up and which, even when you did get it going, seemed only to be able to tune into stations that played classical music or had voices droning on about the news.

Well, I did. I got the radio. And from then on I would keep it next to my bed and listen to my favourite shows and to the cricket. This was South Africa, 1971. There was *Squad Cars* in which allegedly heroic police officers 'protected the people of South Africa' and waited, much to our amusement, 'in fast cars on foot'. I say 'to our amusement' because the announcer got the rhythm all wrong and it wasn't at all clear that there was meant to be a comma between 'fast cars' and 'on foot'. Our games in the garden involved making police cars from cardboard boxes in which we would run around 'on foot'. There was *Check Your Mate*, in which besotted (or sometimes not so besotted) couples would be quizzed on how well they knew their husbands or wives. Does he put his left sock on first or his right? Well? The tension was perfectly bearable, but I loved it anyway. There was *The Men From the Ministry*, an inexplicably popular British sitcom.

And there was the cricket.

No television, you see. That was the thing. South Africa didn't get television until 1975 and not 'properly' until 1976. And even then it wasn't much. Without television there was only radio, and cricket on the radio is something altogether different from cricket on television. I didn't know it then, but I do now. Cricket on the radio is a game of the imagination whereas cricket on television is a matter of fact. Consider, for example, Collingwood's catch in the 2005 one-day series against Australia. When you watch it on TV it beggars belief. But when you listen to it on the radio, it defies imagination. 'Words,' said the commentator, 'cannot do justice to what we have just seen.' And he was right. Words could not, but the silence could. 'Oh my word,' he said, and then he shut up. And in the silence I imagined Collingwood catching a thousand impossible catches, each better than the one before.

It was at Lord's, you see, on a perfect summer's day. The perfect place on the perfect day. It was England against Australia. It was tense, it was glorious and it was the big bully boy Hayden, a man whose wicket is as prized as it is rare. I wasn't there. I forgot to fill in the form to get tickets. But I was listening on the radio. Australia were something ridiculous for three – 50 or 60. Some number anyway which you would never have guessed. Australian scores start at a hundred for one and climb from there. They don't do early order collapses – or not often. But there they were, struggling a bit with England dreaming all sorts of impossible dreams. Harmison came into bowl with his usual unpredictable rhythm. It's the strange thing about Harmison. You watch him run in and you – like, I suspect, him – have no sense of what might be coming. The ball of the century or a tired long hop? Who knows? An unplayable delivery just short of a length that rises so sharply it will catch a tall man in the gullet. Or a ball like the one with which he opened the Ashes series in Australia. A delivery so wide and wild and, well, hopeless, that you sensed, we sensed, even the players sensed in that ghastly moment, that England were doomed.

That was later; this was then. Back at Lord's in 2005 Harmison was the best in the world. He goes up, his left arm leading in that slightly awkward, front-on style he has, and down comes the ball some way short of a length and rising. The word commentators favour for a good Harmison ball is 'steepling', which means it rises faster than it reasonably should. Matthew Hayden, one of the most belligerent and powerful opening bats the game has known, is on strike and he is not the kind to be put off by a little steepling. He can hook and he can cut and he does both with a swaggering violence that suggests a troubled childhood, a disastrous divorce or at the very least a man with a bad headache and a point to prove. You can steeple him all you want. Bring it on. If it's straight at his throat he may treat it with a little respect. But otherwise he is going to hit it. And when he hits the ball, as the saying goes, it stays hit. In this case the ball is not quite at his throat and so he cuts. Brutally. When you cut a fast bowler, the shot uses the pace of the ball and then gives it some. Today Harmison is bowling at a shade under 90 miles an hour. Hayden gives it some. The ball accelerates off the bat in the general direction of Watford. It's going at maybe 100 miles an hour. I don't know. Maybe more. It's going faster than I can throw or run or – for heaven's sake – drive my motorcycle. And clearly it is going too high and too fast for anyone to catch. From the moment it leaves the bat, it looks like a one-bounce four. Except for Paul Collingwood. Collingwood is fielding at his favourite position somewhere between gully and point. Over the years he's made it his own. All the great fielders do. Jonty Rhodes and before him Colin Bland. There are specialist fielders for most positions in cricket. Wicket keeper and slip are obvious ones. You need safe hands, concentration and lightning reactions. But gully or point are more difficult. Partly because the ball travels fastest to those positions. And partly because that's where it is most unpredictable. It spins and turns and slides. It may come off a thick edge and be turning viciously. Or it comes off the face of the bat and screams past you before you've blinked. And it's where batsmen sometimes look for unwise singles, so that an alert fielder gets more opportunities for a run out than at, say, mid-off or square leg. And so the best fielders tend to play there, prowling, alert, threatening. Keeping the batsmen honest. Especially those, like Hayden, who like to cut.

And so Hayden cuts the ball from Harmison. But he doesn't just cut. He doesn't dab it down to third man for a single. What he does is something much more primal, more violent. He slashes at the ball. He really belts it, like it's personal. Like he never wants to see it, or Harmison, again.

'We are they who come faster than fate,' James Elroy Flecker wrote in 'War Song Of The Saracens'. One of those phrases that stuck, somewhere in passing. One of those phrases that you read or hear and you know that sooner or later it will be apt. And now it fits Collingwood like a glove. He has taken some spectacular catches in his time. Think of Ricky Ponting off Panesar or Sangakkara off Jimmy Anderson. But this? This is something else. For this he moves faster than fate. 'You don't see something like this many times in life,' Sir Ian Botham said on the television commentary when I looked it up on YouTube. Collingwood leaps up and away and he's leading with his right, which is to say his wrong, arm. The ball is a little to the left of him. It is past and beyond him before his right hand, which must therefore be travelling faster than the ball, catches up with it. It happens at an incredible speed. Even in slow motion it is hard to understand how it is possible. But there he is. Where the ball merely flies, Collingwood soars. He is Melville's Catskill eagle in *Moby Dick*. 'Even in his lowest swoop, he is still higher than the other birds upon the plain, even though they soar.' And soaring in the sunlit heights, he grabs the ball and...

Well, rather like Icarus when the wax melted, he falls to earth. He has got as close to the gods as it is possible to get and now he has no choice but to come down with a mighty crash. 'The height that he is off the ground,' said Botham, 'is the amazing thing.' Perhaps it is. In retrospect, perhaps, the amazing thing is that Collingwood appears not to feel the impact as he crumples onto the Lord's grass. Try it yourself. Climb on a five-foot-high wall and then fall off. Hold yourself sideways so that your thighs, elbow, chest and chin hit the ground at the same time. It must have hurt like hell, but Colly didn't notice. He didn't die like Icarus. He didn't disappear beneath the waves. The 'expensive, delicate ship' that is a full house at Lord's on a summer's day rose as one to acclaim him. You can see him on television – or, better still, imagine it. He has leapt to an improbable height. His body is twisted the wrong way so that he lands on his chest. His arms are busy with the ball and are not therefore in any position to protect him when he thuds into the ground. His chin may or may not have decked. But he doesn't notice. He doesn't care. He has caught the impossible catch and that is all that matters. He bounces – literally – and then he is up and grinning, ready to accept the adulation of his teammates. I saw the TV replay that night and part of me regrets that I did. Because in my mind it had been as perfect, better even, than it really was. I had filled in the silence myself. I had seen him like I saw Icarus. I had felt the blinding heat of the sun. I had imagined, as perhaps he had imagined, that once his fingers had curled perfectly around the ball, nothing else matters. He could land, he could die – who cared? For Icarus and for Collingwood the coming back is as nothing. It matters not whether it will be possible to do it again. What matters is the one, perfect golden moment. And the landing? The landing can take care of itself.

Spare a thought (but only a small one) for Matthew Hayden. The laws of cricket are clear. A batsman who is out must go. No questions. He is not allowed to hang around the crease. If he does, he will be charged with dissent and fined. And now Hayden doesn't go immediately. Not because he is having a strop. Not out of dissent. But because, like all of us, he can't quite believe what has just happened. He stays rooted in disbelief to his spot. He closes his eyes as though he hopes to wake up and find he has been dreaming. 'For death was a difficult trade, and the sword was a broker of doom,' says the poem. It is a curiosity of cricket, of which more later, that the very act which brings glory – the hitting of the ball – is also the act that brings your downfall. 'Cricket only works,' Bob Woolmer told me, 'if you hit the ball.' But cricketers so often fail precisely because they hit the ball. I don't know what the averages are, but I would guess that 30 or 40 per cent of all cricketing dismissals (it's more, the worse the standard of play) are from catches. Your sword is ever the broker of your doom. It is something we all know too well. Only last Saturday I was caught – for the third time this season – at deep mid-wicket. And it is only the third innings of the season. Three times in. Three times out – and each time it is my bat, it is me, it is the desire to hit that brings my downfall. So spare that thought for Hayden. He had hit a cracking shot – and he is out. No fault of his own. How was he to know that Collingwood had recently learned to fly? Only when he recovers from his momentary shock does he turn, tuck his bat under his arm and begin his slow, disbelieving walk to the Pavilion. Later I saw all this on television, but the first time I had to imagine it. I can imagine him as he goes. At Lord's the

TV replay screen is at the far end of the ground, so that departing batsmen have to watch the replays over their shoulders. Hayden doesn't look back. Perhaps he's afraid of what he will do. If he saw the catch again he wouldn't believe it. He would say there was no way Collingwood could have caught that and therefore he cannot possibly be out.

But the point is that I remember Collingwood's catch with an intensity that would alarm my girlfriend if ever I admitted to it. I remember it the way I remember lines of poetry, but perhaps this is to be expected. It has a rhythm and metre and rhyme all of its own. It has multiple meanings for multiple occasions. It pops into my head at opportune moments. And inopportune ones, come to think of it. For cricket became poetry and poetry was cricket. It lit a fire in my imagination and in that moment became a portable companion to my life. I relive it during dull dinner parties. It reminds of what it was to be young. It gives me something to think about when there is no one there to talk to. And, in part, it does this because the first time I saw it was in my head. Like sex, the first time was imaginary. And, not quite like sex, it was better even than being there.

But these were not thoughts I was ready to share with my daughter's new boyfriend. Not yet. Not in so many words.

I LOVE …

Cricket's silences (and others, come to that)

Fortunately not many words are required. He gives 'taciturn' new meaning. He makes quiet seem noisy. In the conversational stakes he gives a sleeping possum a run for its money. 'Thank you' is his equivalent of telling his life story. 'Thanks' is a doctoral dissertation. 'Ta' is just about par for the course. And absolute silence is what we have come to expect. It's not that he doesn't converse. It's just that he doesn't say anything while he's doing it. He smiles. He nods. He frowns. His eyebrows wander around his gentle expressive face like caterpillars in search of a leaf. He shrugs. He uses his hands to point at the Marmite or the salt or the water or whatever else his long athletic body needs to keep him going for another ten minutes before it needs to be fed again. And mostly he looks embarrassed. Embarrassed to be here. Embarrassed to be in love. But words? Not a chance.

So much so that my girlfriend has started to see me in a new light. For twenty years she has thought of me as the silent one. For twenty years she has joked about my unwillingness to chat. Sometimes, to make a point, she has entire conversations with the wall. There's a painting in the kitchen, the work of a friend, that she finds particularly sympathetic as a conversational partner. She and it are in complete agreement on all subjects. And in the unlikely event that they do disagree, she always manages to win it round. 'Don't you think?' she says and the painting knows better than to disagree. Me too, but I haven't said anything anyway. But compared to the boy I am garrulous to the point of exhaustion. I am a storm to his drizzle. I am Niagara to his dripping tap.

Shyness, you see. That's my excuse and I have no doubt whatsoever it is his as well. I recognise the symptoms. I understand the fringe. I know just how useful it can be for something to hide behind. When I had hair I had a fringe. I was an acutely shy boy and I became an obliquely shy man. My high-school report said (and I quote; it stung) that I 'retreated into silence when assailed by the more mundane comments of [my] contemporaries'. Nowadays I can't remember why it stung. It seems pretty accurate to me, except that actually I was silent long before my contemporaries assailed me with their more mundane comments. There was no need for me to retreat. I was already there. Contemplating the passing scene from the quieter recesses of my mind. Buried in my books somewhere. Nursing my Achilles tendon. Learning poetry by heart on the off-chance I could spout it to a passing girl.

Of course his silence applies only to us. Left alone with our daughter, he is transformed. The ice with her was presumably broken during the early encounters at the skate park. Despite several imaginative lines of inquiry into his knowledge of the constellations of the Northern Hemisphere, I have no clue of how he went about sweet-talking her.

'Ah, the stars,' I say one evening. The stars are sadly not visible. 'I remember learning the names of all the constellations when I was a boy.'

'Oh,' he says. Not even 'Oh?' Just 'Oh'. The conversational equivalent of a forward defensive prod if ever I saw one. The ball trickles to point 'and there's no run there'.

I secretly suspect it was the other way round. I suspect she sweet-talked him, for it is well known that in these high and far-off times (oh best beloved) it is not necessarily the boy who makes the moves. It is perfectly possible that she took matters into her own hands. In any case, whatever shyness he felt with her in those early weeks quickly disappeared. Perhaps it is the freedom MSN gives. Perhaps it is the liberation of texting. Personally I have always found texting inadequate to the task of expressing the multiple subtleties of my thought. Texting doesn't do irony. Texting doesn't allow for the dry humour to which I aspire. But perhaps he has no such burden. Perhaps he has only one thought… In any case, I know that when we are not there he is a man transformed. Like some men on the cricket field.

Jimmy Anderson comes to mind. Journalists complain when they are sent to interview him. He is a man for whom one word is a soundbite. Three a speech. Interviewing him is hard work. But put him in the middle, with a new ball in his hand and the wind at his back, and he's a new man. Suddenly some dark beast wells within him. Ask Daniel Flynn, the New Zealand batsman. The umbrellas were just going up at Lord's on the first day of the 2008 Lord's Test against the Black Caps when Anderson banged in a short ball at Flynn. It was a very good bouncer. It was a highly aggressive bouncer. It was not what you would expect if you met Jimmy Anderson in the street. If you met Jimmy in the street you would think he is a lovely young man. Quiet. Polite. Just how you like them. But on a cricket field? Flynn responded in kind. He stepped back and across (good man) and tried to pull it for four. But it was too high and too quick for him. He played too late, missed and (are you listening, Bob Woolmer?) the ball clattered into the grille of his helmet – so hard that it buckled the titanium and knocked out a tooth. Causing Flynn, according to one newspaper report, to 'feel unwell'. Yes, well, you would, wouldn't you?

So removing us has a comparable effect on the young man. When we're not there he chats with my daughter. He whispers sweet somethings to her. He laughs, he flirts. Flirts! I heard him laughing with her when they thought no one was listening. They were in the kitchen hunting for the chocolates I had hidden on the top shelf.

'Damn,' said my daughter. 'They must be here somewhere.'

'You don't need chocolates.' he said. 'You've got me.'

I made a mental note to buy more chocolates. And not to hide them. To reverse the equation, you understand. 'You don't need him, you've got chocolates.' And then I walked into the kitchen. It was marginally less embarrassing than being found loitering in the hallway.

'Hello,' I said.

'Hello, Dad,' said my daughter.

But her young man said nothing at all. Instead he went the red that Jimmy Anderson used to dye his hair when he first broke into the England team and before he grew up.

Early on my daughter advised me to talk about sport, but in the tension of the early meetings I have forgotten. Instead I have tried the weather. As a bonding mechanism this has not been a great success.

'Hello,' I say.

'Yeah, alright.' (Don't worry; I'm getting used to it. Sometimes I even manage not to grimace.)

'You're not skating today?'

'Too wet.'

'Oh.'

Other conversations flame, burn, take one quick turn and are gone. Someone once said that about James Dean and the comparison is not wholly inappropriate. The boy may not be a rebel, but he certainly seems to lack a cause.

'England played badly again.' (This is me being Renaissance man. I am talking about football, not cricket. As England manager, Steve McLaren is not held to have been a great success.)

'Yeah.'

'I don't know what happens to them. People play like champs for their club and then like rabbits for England.'

'Yeah.'

'You don't play football?'

'No.'

Oh.

We are at dinner. We've known the boy for all of ten days or, as my girlfriend puts it, eighteen words. It's raining again. Too wet for skateboarding. He and my daughter have spent the day in the West End. Taking advantage of the free transport so thoughtfully provided by our mayor. In an attempt to impress me, she drags him to the National Gallery and the Science Museum.

'How was the gallery?' I ask.

'Boring,' he says.

Hmmm. Still, worth another go.

'Boring, how?' I ask. My version of another go. I try to ignore the slight edge in my voice. Perhaps he does too.

'Dead boring.'

Hmmm.

The Science Museum fares marginally better. He tells me about the rhythmic pounding of the pistons of the steam turbine in the main hall. 'Real smooth,' he says. 'Going in and out.'

Hmmm. I have nothing to say to this.

'Leave them alone,' says my girlfriend. 'Give them time.'

She's right, of course, and I declare a unilateral truce. I will leave them alone. I will give them time. They use this time to excuse themselves and disappear upstairs where, they claim, they are watching a DVD. I look around for some cigarette cards, but I forgot to collect any. I doubt very much my family's South African stamps, 1897–1963, which I seem to have acquired, will do the trick. Perhaps I should invest in some model steam engines. Or chocolate.

The following Monday I answer the door when he rings the bell.

'Hello,' I say.

'Yeah, alright.'

My cricket bat is in the hall. I pick it up and practise a couple of forward defensive strokes. High elbow. Left foot well forward. By rights this should be an unmissable opportunity for him to ask about the weekend before. In my fantasy world the conversation goes something like this:

> *'Have a good game'? he asks.*
>
> *'Not too bad,' I reply. 'Got a scratchy 50.'* (This early modesty won't last. In a minute I'll tell him about the three

consecutive fours I hit off the opposition quickie, the one who claimed once to have played for the Trinidad Under 19s. Just need to find the right adjectives. 'Classic' is a bit too prosaic. 'Sumptuous'? That's more like it. Three sumptuous off drives. Also that it was scratchy only compared to the most fluent innings of, say, David Gower in his pomp. And watching Gower in his pomp was a thousand times more elegant and a million times more 'smooth' than watching some gleaming pistons pumping 'in and out' at the Science Museum.)

'Well done. Did you win?'

'Oh yes, did I not say that? A match-winning innings. We were 38 for six when I got to the wicket, chasing 103 to win. I made 52 of the missing 65 runs.' (Of course none of this is true, but my feeling about fantasy is that if you go down that road at all, you might as well go the whole way.)

'That's good. I wish I played cricket. You always sound like you have such fun.' (The fantasy is kicking in big time now.)

'You should come. You'd be welcome at the club.' (I'll save the bit about needing someone to carry the drinks until later.)

'Thanks, that would be great. But I don't know if she will come with me.'

'She'll come if you do.' (A recurring fantasy, using the boy wonder to get my daughter interested in cricket. It's her dotage I'm worried about. How will she spend her twilight years if not wrapped in a warm blanket watching Middlesex eke out a wholly undeserved Division 2 end-of-season, meaningless draw at Southgate? Some friends of ours have a daughter of roughly the same age. Since she was eight she has enthusiastically donned her whites and

gone out to play cricket for her school(s) and for a club. Where did we go wrong? Where did they go right? Is it because their daughter is an only child? What curious alchemy delivered such a girl? But then they told me the other day she has met a boy and given up cricket completely. Now she spends her days buried in an iPod or his arms or – which is worse – both at the same time. Even at mealtimes. I should count my blessings.)

'Take any catches?'

'Only three.' (This has now entered truly fantasy land. I last got three catches in a match in 1973 and one of those I caught only because the ball went up my sleeve and lodged in my armpit. I have a scar where the stitching cut me.)

'Excellent! You must be very good.'

(Yes, alright, I admit this fantasy thing is getting out of hand.)

But of course these conversations never happen. Nothing is quite so uninteresting as the details of someone else's cricketing fortune. Recall Kit Wright's beautiful verse, 'Cricket Widow': *'Out of the love you bear me, / By all its sweet beginnings, / Darling heart, please spare me / The details of your innings.'* What actually happens is this: I play a couple of shots. He watches me the same way ice-cream-licking kids watch an elephant in the zoo. The elephant is, you know, kind of interesting in an exotic sort of way, what with the wrinkly bum and the different-sized tusks, the pathetically small bottom lip and the fact that they have toenails and do droppings the size of footballs.

But when it comes down to it, the kids are really only there for the ice cream.

There's a brief silence.

'Is she in?' he says. He means the ice cream.

The ice cream has been in for some time. Washing her hair. Dyeing her hair. I may not have mentioned this but the boy has borderline goth tastes. Not, as my daughter put it, 'goth goth'. But still, *goth-ish*. T-shirts with skulls on them. Belts with studs on them. Tight black jeans. Goth with a bit of Iron Maiden thrown in. Bullet For My Valentine. As a consequence (actually I am not completely sure about the cause-and-effect relationship; after all, the boy hasn't done the same) my daughter has dyed her hair black. My girlfriend (who is herself prone to bouts of orange or magenta and who did not manage to get through her teenage years without going through a 'black' period, despite the fact that she has the most gorgeous blonde hair for which many women and not a few men would kill) is wholly approving. I am not.

'Say nothing,' counsels my girlfriend.

'Why?' I ask my daughter. My version of 'saying nothing'. I make a little speech about the blessings of blonde hair and the putative millions of women who would kill for it.

'You wouldn't understand,' she says.

'I told you,' says my girlfriend.

The boy is watching me curiously. It takes me a moment to remember his question.

'Yes,' I say. The ice cream is in.

Only I don't say the second part.

'I'll go up then,' he says.

'Nice to see you.'

'Yeah.'

He 'goes up', meaning to her bedroom, the one where his visiting hours cease at the midnight hour.

Perhaps it's just as well. Actually what happened at the

weekend was I got out for a duck, caught at mid-wicket, dropped a sitter while fielding at mid-off and when the skipper, in an act of early-season charity (the league had not yet begun) brought me on to bowl two overs, I got hit for sixteen runs. As against that, I did get the wicket of their big scorer. Last man out, caught while attempting injudiciously to hit me – not the ball, me; remember in cricket it's always personal – to somewhere near Brighton. He had a row about it afterwards. The scorer had written 'caught at cow' in the scorebook. The player was keen to point out that deep mid-wicket and 'cow' are not, repeat NOT, the same thing.

'In what sense?' said the scorer.

'Cow,' said the big hitter, still padded up (he had gone to check the scorebook before he had even removed his pads), 'is where you hit it if your right hand pushes through too much. Deep mid-wicket is where you stroke a full delivery on middle and leg.'

'I thought I saw some right hand,' said the scorer. He was a lot bigger than the big hitter.

'What I do with my right hand is my business,' said the big hitter. He tried to seize the scorebook to make the necessary amendment, but the scorer wasn't having any of it.

It was hard not to smile, so I didn't bother.

In the absence of the boy (who has 'gone up', though not in my estimation), I practise a couple more defensive prods until I see myself in the mirror. And then I stop. Whom do I think I'm kidding?

I LOVE…

The amateur game

He has a name, but I won't trouble you with it. You would only look him up on YouTube and what good would that do? It wouldn't tell you anything. You would see him cutting up Parliament Square on his skateboard or performing a five-oh on the South Bank to the consternation of tourists and the delight of his equally floppy-haired, bedraggled-jeans, pimple-faced inarticulate mates. Perhaps you would go straight to the clip of 'best bails' and chuckle as he lands, time after time, on his scrawny backside, a sheepish grin on his face and another rip or two in his dirty, hanging crotch, beltless, jailhouse jeans. Perhaps, like me, you would be impressed, for it turns out he is quite good at skateboarding. Good enough for him and his mates to have a collective name and a modest following. They have a sponsor and they use the money to buy kit and to put up videos of themselves on the web. He is the star of the group. I have been on YouTube and I have watched him performing his tricks (and failing to perform them) and I have marvelled. He does things that do not at first or even second glance look possible.

But he knows nothing about cricket. I try him with the

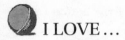

story of Collingwood's catch. Nothing. I mention Harmison's first ball in the just completed, disastrous 2006–2007 Ashes series. Nothing. He shrugs, like it doesn't matter. Like it's something that happened far away in a country of which we know little. In desperation I try telling a tale of my own exploits.

Only last season I was involved in a tense match against a side from west London. There we were, 247 for four off our 45 overs and they were drawing ever closer. With ten overs to go, they needed 45 runs and had four wickets in hand. Five overs to go, they needed nineteen, but had lost another wicket. Then two wickets fell in quick succession. In came the doughty old performer who played for Middlesex in the sixties and still cuts a sprightly figure. He's a bowler, though, not a batsman. Tall and earnest and blinking to keep the dust out of his contact lenses. A sort of Bob Willis figure. Beaked nose. Downturned mouth. In our innings he took a couple of wickets, but mostly he kept it tidy. Hard to score off. Always just outside off stump. Always just short of a length. Not much pace to his bowling these days, but he still gets a bit of bounce. Just enough to make the batsman pay attention. As a batsman, he looks very correct. You can imagine him driving. You can't imagine him hooking, not since the hips started giving him grief. But there he was, taking guard and looking round meaningfully. I am never sure whether batsmen remember what they see when they look around to check out the field placings. The assumption is that they are doing it because they will then

a) know where not to hit catches and
b) be able, like Graham Thorpe at his best, to steer the ball between the fielders and get runs that should never

> have been scored. I know that when I go out to bat I make a point of reciting the field settings to myself to the rhythm of one of those GI marching songs. You know the form: 'There's a man there at point *duh-duh-duh da dnnhh*. And two in the slips *duh-duh-duh da dnnhh*. Don't hit to square leg *duh-duh-duh da dnnhh*. Best back past his head *duh-duh-duh da dnnhh*.' I also know that the minute the bowler begins his run up, I forget everything I have just said and try to hit him over cow corner.

But perhaps that's just me.

So there we are, a tense game in a Middlesex lower division knockout match. Our west London opponents need ten off the last two overs. We only need one wicket. The tall guy's partner at the other end is a mouthy fifteen-year-old. Gave me a bit of lip when we were batting. Shouted 'Come on, old man' when I was struggling to pull on my gloves with my teeth. Told the bowler to slow down so I could see the ball after I played and missed. That sort of lip. Probably playing his first senior game. This is a cup game, knockout, and so we're not about to let up on him. It's a new over and the kid has to face. Westy tosses the ball to Zoobs, who comes thundering in from the lower end of the pitch. Our club ground is very pretty. It's set in a leafy glade in north London. It has a drainage problem and quickly becomes unplayable in wet weather. But today is dry. So Zoobs bowls and he does it well. Fast, short, straight. Dot ball follows dot ball. The kid is scared witless, no doubt about it. The third ball hits him on the glove. The fourth ball goes whistling past his ears. He adjusts his helmet strap. He's seen what happens when people get hit on the head. The helmet gives you some protection, but it's still not much fun. The fifth ball is pitched up. It smacks him on the pads. It's as plumb as plumb can be. Halfway up middle stump, well back in his crease. We all appeal to the rafters. Players two grounds away look over to see what has happened. Doogs and The Undertaker are already celebrating our victory. 'Not out,' says the(ir) umpire. 'Going down leg side.' Like hell it was. Even from my position at backward point I can see he's out. Chuntering grumpily, we resume our positions.

Zoobs steams in from the other end. It's a decent ball. The kid isn't even looking as he jumps to get out the way. The ball catches the shoulder of his bat and flies over Matt's head for four.

Doogs has to bowl the last over. They need five to tie, six to win. We need that wicket. First ball and all the old guy who used to bowl for Middlesex can do is block it. Second ball is full outside off stump. He slashes at it. It sails through to deep cover where Atters is patrolling the boundary. The old guy wants to settle for one, but there is no way the kid is going to face another ball. 'Yes!' he yells. Atters throws it in – but to the wrong end. The old guy scrapes in before Doogs can hurl it to the other end. Four balls to go, four needed. The old guy on strike. Doogs bowls, a slower one on middle stump. The old guy swipes again, but miscues it completely. Instead of shooting off to cow corner for a match-winning four, the ball catches the edge of the bat and shoots up 50 or 60 feet... towards me at point. Towards, but not to. I set off at a blistering (well, I had blisters) pace. I'm running at an angle so that when I get to the ball I won't be looking directly into the sun. The rest of the team are watching. I hear shouts of 'Catch!' and 'Yours!' I feel the wind in my ears and the sun on my face. I remember what it was to be young. How scary it was. How I always needed to pee at the wrong moment. How embarrassing it was the last time I dropped a catch. At the last moment the ball seems to swerve in the air. I have to check my run and dive to the left. A relatively simple two-hander turns into a last-chance left-handed dive. I'm on the 'square', which is baked hard by the July sun. As I land a cloud of dust and grass flies up my nose. My glasses fall off… And miraculously, the ball sticks. And (like Collingwood?) I am in that moment oblivious to pain. And (like Collingwood? This is nice; I like being 'like Collingwood'. It has a certain ring to it. It speaks of a limitless athleticism) I bounce up to receive the accolades of my teammates.

'I never doubted you for a minute,' lies the skipper. You can see the doubt washing off him, the way mud slides off in the shower. It is only that evening that I notice a yard of skin is missing from my left shoulder and I seem, inexplicably, to be bleeding from a hole in my chin.

My daughter's boyfriend tries to look interested. He really does. I can see him nodding in all the right places. Every now and then he glances at her as if to ask, 'Am I doing okay?' She nods encouragingly. He smiles at me.

And he couldn't care less.

He has managed to survive thirteen years of English state education without ever once being required to play any sport at all and particularly not cricket. Not for him the timeless (timeless? I mean it ironically) rhythms of A. E. Housman's Shropshire childhood. Unhappy in love, Housman remembers how

Twice a week the winter thorough
Here I stood to keep the goal:

Football then was fighting sorrow
For the young man's soul.

Now in Maytime to the wicket
Out I march with bat and pad:
See the son of grief at cricket
Trying to be glad.

Football was the winter sport, cricket the summer. And the transition comes in May, when the pitches dry out and the grass is growing and Larkin's trees are now fully in leaf. Always had been. Always would be.

It's a good time for my daughter. She has exams later in the year, but she is not unduly threatened by them. The evenings are growing longer and these early summer evenings are times of infinite promise. You can trace the arcs of their length. Each day the sun sets a minute or two later and each minute feels like a gift. A moment plucked from the abyss otherwise known as the night. A moment to be shared with someone you love.

Her boy was born around the time of the poll tax riots, Thatcher's child. He entered the school system just as that most avid of cricket fans, John Major, was deciding to sell off as many playing fields as he could. In a particularly revealing moment, Major later said it was the policy he most regretted. Mind you; I wouldn't want to be hard on Major. He secured his forgiveness on leaving Downing Street where, in what I presume was a wholly calculated but nonetheless highly effective gesture, he told the press that he was 'off to the Oval to watch cricket'.

The boy therefore entered a schooling system in which

sport played little part. Hard to believe, but true. My own childhood had been filled with sport. At secondary school, once my tendon had healed, I played sport seven days out of seven. Always hard, always to win. It didn't much matter what sport, as long as it wasn't rugby. I would play pretty much anything with a ball. Even water polo, which made rugby look like a vicar's tea party. The point was to play and, if possible, to win. But my daughter's boyfriend fell into that gap between the playing fields of Eton and the target-driven, league-table-obsessed, obesity-fearing national curriculum we have now. His dad wasn't much of a one for sport, and therefore he had to make it up for himself. Hence, perhaps, his interest in skateboarding. Skateboarding can be 'learned on the job'. It requires no facilities, no coaching and very little outlay of cash. It doesn't need teams or leagues or an organising committee. There are no ladders or friendly matches and definitely no old farts in blazers. It is the street sport par excellence. Its roots are in the counterculture of 1970s West Coast USA where boys began to surf the empty swimming pools of winter just as they, or their friends, had surfed the summer waves. It has a language all of its own. It is cheap, rebellious and imbued with a sense of invention, creativity and freedom. It offers limited but sufficient opportunities for conflict with the law.

In *The Cricket Match*, his minor classic from 1924, Hugh de Selincourt offers a mournful assessment of the charms of football over cricket: 'The lads were mad about football. In season and out and the season itself now began in August. And no blame to them! Off with your jackets: four decent goal-posts ready at once: Here's a footer: nothing else wanted. The more the merrier. No old 'uns need apply. Dribble and hack and punt and charge about. Sweat, and enjoy yourselves.'

It is the same with skateboarding. Sweat and swoop and no old 'uns need apply. And it can sometimes, just sometimes, be amazing. All sports have such moments, when the technique and timing and circumstance combine to produce the perfect shot, or pass, or save, or ball or, should you be a skateboarder, the perfect 180 frontside ollie. And in that moment, no matter the sport, the protagonist stands at the far golden edge of human achievement, as close to the gods as you can get without actually dying. And so I find I am glad about the skateboarding. It is not my sport, but it is a sport. And with that in common, with the language of the golden moments, we must surely find something to say to each other? He will talk about his favourite moves. I shall discourse loftily on the joys of the back-foot off drive. We shall at no stage mention my daughter. All will be well.

It's just a question of balance, that's all.

I LOVE …

That you get what you deserve

I know. I know. He's nothing to do with me. You don't have to tell me. I should keep out of it. I should leave them alone. And I would. Only she's my daughter. And he does seem to be 'around' rather a lot. He comes 'around' of an evening. He appears late on Friday nights. He is 'around' early on Saturday mornings. He is often at meals. And he is clearly more than a brief romance. It's been what – a month now? Six weeks? Plus the weeks before we met him. An eternity when you're fifteen. Sorry, sixteen. Annie and I knew each other for fully 36 hours and for years afterwards I counted that as a relationship. It seems only polite to get to know him a little.

'No, really, Dad, you don't have to,' says my daughter. She has that steely tone of voice, the one she used to use when she didn't want to go to bed at the appointed hour.

'Well, I mean,' I say.

I agree this is not the most convincing argument.

'I'm just being polite.'

This is not wholly convincing either.

'And he might learn something.'

This is wholly unconvincing. But then our arguments are often like this.

That night after supper we are sitting at the dining-room table. We are now six, not five. It is early summer, a warm enough day for the time of year. Nobody has much to say. Instead we watch the darkness settle on the garden and listen to the sounds of the neighbourhood shutting itself in for the night. Next door has recently acquired a ping-pong table but now there are the sounds of balls being stowed. The last ping has ponged. Next door but one the baby is crying. It is not a distressed cry. It is an 'I-will-soon-be-asleep' whimper. A sound that all is as it should be. It's been a tiring day. Next door but two is yelling for the cat to come and get his food. The cat appears not to be interested. Either he has killed something itself or he has smelled the scent of one of the foxes that seem to have made a home in the gardens behind us. In any case he's not coming. Next door but two gives up and goes inside. There is the sound of the back door closing. My girlfriend rises to close ours as well.

'Any plans?' I say. It's a general invitation, meant specifically for my daughter and her boy.

'Um,' says my daughter.

I know that 'um'. She's been using it since she was very little. It is the sound of a tricky question on its way. Her boy seems to know it too. He has developed an almost obsessive interest in the middle distance.

'Um, Dad? Are you busy next week?'

'Not especially. Why?'

'I was thinking, it would be nice to go to some galleries and stuff. I really want to see more art.'

'Okay, sure. Good. I'll be happy to go with you. Does he...?'

But she's too quick for that. She doesn't want any questions about whether 'he' wants to come with us.

'Cool! Thanks, Dad,' she says. And then (in case I hadn't realised), 'You're the best. By the way, I was wondering, would it be okay if he stays here tonight?'

'He' is now concentrating on the picture, the one my girlfriend finds it so entertaining to talk to when I am being taciturn. My girlfriend, meanwhile, has finished closing up at the back.

'Sure, honey,' she says. 'We can make up the spare bed.'

'Oh, yes, right,' I say. 'The spare bed. We can make up the spare bed.'

My daughter looks relieved, like we have given the best answer. If I were a more suspicious man I would think she and my girlfriend had already caucused this particular decision. My girlfriend always did favour a pre-caucus caucus. It makes it so much easier to get the right result. And you don't even have to cheat in writing the minutes.

'Thanks, Dad. We'll be back later. We're going out to the Heath now,' says my daughter.

'Yeah, alright,' says her boy.

'Bye,' I say to the slamming door.

Of course I shouldn't get all antsy about the 'yeah, alright'. It's a phrase I use myself at the beginning of the cricket season. Everybody does. Sometime in late March or early April people start gathering at the club. These are mostly people I hardly know, apart from cricket. We're there to get things going for the new season. The nets need repairing. The artificial pitch needs to be cleaned. The winter moss and algae and bird droppings need to be scraped off. The boundary rope needs repairs. There are trees at the northern end that need pruning. The sign with our sponsor's name (don't be fooled; the presence of a sponsor speaks volumes not about our ability as cricketers, but about the fact that one of our number occupies a senior position in the sponsor's firm) needs touching up. And there is work to be done in the clubhouse too. A bit of carpentry. A spot of paint. And – most important – repairs to the protective mesh over the clubhouse windows. It is characteristic of our club – it seems to apply to a lot of clubs – that someone inadvertently built the clubhouse at what is popularly known as 'cow corner'. I am not sure of the etymology of the phrase. Suffice it to say that if you hit a cricket ball with as much power and as little technique as possible, cow corner is where it will go. It is the point somewhere between midwicket (where a proper leg-side shot will go) and mid-on (where an even more proper leg-side shot will go). It is the first (and often last) resort of batsmen in a hurry or of batsmen facing less than challenging bowling. It goes without saying that in the autumn of my cricketing ability, 'cow' is where I score most of my runs and where I most often get out.

Only last season I made a memorable 49 against excruciatingly slow bowling served up by a commander of the Metropolitan Police. Pie chucking of the worst sort. Catch him in the bar later and he will give you a lot of old rot about line and length. Delusional nonsense. These were lollies, pure and simple. The only line they had was down leg and the only length was something short of the 22 yards. If the keeper wanted to take them he'd have to stand in front of the stumps. The innings was memorable only because it was played mostly in driving rain in a dismal public ground in north-west London and because I didn't play a single scoring shot on the off side.

I did, however, hit several boundaries in the vicinity of cow corner. Needless to say I was out stumped trying to reach my 50 with a six which, had I connected, would have landed somewhere near Brent Cross shopping centre.

But I didn't.

It was, Rob said, 'typical'. Recently I had to send him a note promising, on pain of voluntary deselection, that I would not get myself out, caught at cow, more than one innings in three. As I write, this promise is under some strain. I have been out three times this season. On all three occasions I have been caught at cow. To make my promise good I have more or less not to get out that way for the rest of the season. I don't think it is physically possible. There are technical reasons why I hit so many shots in the direction of cow. There are technical reasons why I hit so many of them in the air. But I am not a technician (that's one reason for a start). I am a poet, and so I prefer the poetic explanation. I do it because I like it. It is a comfortable and (when it works) infinitely pleasurable shot.

The opposite of technical is natural. A mighty hoick over cow follows the natural line of the body rather than the line of the ball. The left hand leads, the right hand comes through and (assuming you have kept your balance) the bat ends somewhere over your left shoulder. Like a forehand cross-court in tennis, only the ball travels faster and goes further. And (getting back to cricket) if you connect with the sweet spot of your bat, it is a delight. And it pisses the bowler off no end. They say that the pleasure in batting is in the stroke, in the satisfying crack of leather on willow. But I'll tell you another truth. Part of the pleasure in batting is scoring off bad shots – and then laughing at the bowler.

Technique, on the other hand, is not natural. That's what

makes it technical. It is something you have to learn. You have to make your stroke subservient not to the flow of your body but to the line of the ball. You have to cede that much control – respect, even – to the bowler. It will, in the end, give you far better results. But is cricket really about results? Cricket is poetry and poetry is emotion. And emotion is fluid, dynamic and unpredictable.

'Yeah, alright?' we say as we gather for the new season. Some may go a little further. They may tell you about their work or their wives or girlfriends or their holidays in Bermuda. But on the whole a simple 'Yeah, alright?' will do it. It is an acknowledgement that we are all in this together. It means the season is upon us.

It means things can begin.

She looks so grown up I sometimes forget she is still at school. I blame the uniforms. Or the lack of them. A kid in uniform is still clearly a kid. A kid not in uniform – why, it could be anyone.

But every now and then we get reminded. Today is a Friday. Fridays have become a bit of an emotional rollercoaster recently. On good Fridays 'he' is coming to visit. On bad Fridays 'he' is not available. Today we do not know which it will be because my daughter has had her telephone confiscated at school. The school authorities are admirably strict about this, and when she is caught texting in class, the phone is taken away. She claims innocence. She maintains she was using the calculator but the teacher was having none of it. And so she has no idea whether the boy is coming. Now at her school, when phones are confiscated the parents have to go in and collect them. Again, admirably strict. The school knows that parents will be more determined in disciplining their child if the parents – and not only the child – have to pay a price.

So it is that about four in the afternoon I find myself standing in Student Services getting my – it should be her, but trust me it is my – dressing down. Did I realise how disruptive it was for children to use the telephones in class? Did I share the sense of insult the teacher would have felt? Was I prepared to take steps to make sure it didn't happen again? Was I not personally to blame for the general collapse of standards in the country? And, even as I am pleading guilty – 'yes, sorry, it won't happen again' – to all of the above, I notice my daughter out of the corner of my eye. She – unlike me – has more pressing engagements. She – unlike me – does not feel personally responsible for the decline of modern Britain. What she feels is an urgent need to know if the boy is coming 'to ours' tonight. And so she starts texting.

'I'm sorry,' I say to the deputy headteacher.

'Yes, well, aren't we all,' she replies.

Well, no, not really. Because even I know what it is like to fall in love. I know its fragility. I know its peaks and its troughs.

And it is clear that our daughter's happiness is the happiness of a woman in love. It is so fragile. It breaks in the slightest wind. It appears out of nothingness. Later that evening we are at supper. She mopes. Everything is gloom. Her exams are causing stress and her hair is all wrong. Her eczema is playing up again, she has no nice clothes, she's not hungry. When we ask, 'What's the matter?', she replies, 'Nothing.' When we offer her more food she shakes her head.

'Why don't we go to a movie?' says my girlfriend.

Our daughter doesn't feel like it.

We could invite some people over?

No.

She could give X or Y a call. Maybe they're doing something?

Uh-uh.

We could get drunk and listen to Leonard Cohen?

Only we don't have to resort to that because there is a little buzzing noise in her pocket. Out comes the phone (normally absolutely forbidden at mealtimes) and she reads the text. She holds it up for me to see. 'Am coming,' it says. The two most precious words she knows. Suddenly her world view changes. All is sweetness and light. The great grey clouds massing in the west clear to leave a sparkling sky. A warm orange glow fills the room. The sun's rays float across the Heath to our house on the hill. Can she have seconds? Is there more salad? She even remembers to ask if it is okay if 'he' – no need to say who 'he' is – stays over.

My girlfriend and I exchange glances. We have long since agreed to restrain our more jaded view of the world and to refrain from mentioning heartache, pain, betrayal, loss... all the corollaries of love. I mean, not that this has been my experience. Or not often. But I read books. I watch movies. I know how it ends. Our daughter, though, doesn't believe it will ever end.

'Look at you,' she says. Meaning me and my girlfriend. We exchange those glances and swallow our doubts.

She protects him the way a top order batsman will shield a tail ender. And who can blame her? She knows my quirks. She has spent a lifetime – a short life, but a life nonetheless – navigating each eccentricity. She knows when to push and when to walk away. She wants me to like him. From time to time I hear her explaining us – but mostly me – to him.

'He's foreign,' she says. Meaning me. A catch-all explanation. 'He', by contrast, is not foreign. In this gorgeous, raucous, mongrel nation, he is as English as it is possible to be. Distilled through generations of yeoman stock. Not a Londoner, but from the Midlands. Even my daughter is surprised. At some point she goes to the wedding of one of his family. 'The cousins!' she said. 'There were hundreds of them.'

There are hundreds of us Londoners too, but we come from all over. Six in ten of us were born outside London and four in ten were born outside the country altogether. I have lived here more than half my life and regard myself as English. But I know I could transplant myself to another country without too much trouble. I know that my sense of belonging is held together by a rope of sand whereas for him – England is all there has ever been.

It is clear that she is hopelessly, delightfully, gorgeously in love. She shines when he arrives and fades when he's away. My girlfriend worries about this. She's not convinced of the politics of it. She thinks it is healthy not to dote too much. She thinks it does men – she means me – good to feel insecure.

'He dotes on her too,' I say.

'Early days,' says my girlfriend. 'We'll see.'

But it's clear that he does. He barely says anything, at least not to me. But you have only to watch them walking down the road, their hands lightly brushing until they can get round the corner and out of sight and hold hands properly, to know that for both of them this is a magical, new, life-affirming thing. He has other nice ways of showing it. My daughter's wall of pictures has a slightly different feel. There are train tickets to record each time he has visited. There are newsagent cards with corny messages. There are ticket stubs from gigs they have attended. He buys her little chocolates with pink ribbons and the ribbons go up on the wall.

'They deserve each other,' I say.

It is the golden rule of all sports that you get what you deserve. Not necessarily in that moment, but over time. Someone drops you on nought and you go on to make a half century? Good for you. Your teammate calls you back for a ludicrous second run when you're on 49? It happens. There was a game I played recently. Our batsman at the non-striker's end called for a silly run. His partner sent him back. The fielder swooped in from short mid-wicket and threw the ball underhand at the wicket. It missed. The fielder running round from mid-off to back up snagged his foot on the grass. He tripped and slid. The ball, which would otherwise have gone for four overthrows, hit his heel and bounced back into the wicket. My teammate was out by inches. I was umpiring at the time. You could see on his face he was running through his entire vocabulary of swear words to find something to suit the occasion. Nothing came. No words to describe how he felt. About his partner sending him back. About the relief that the throw missed. About the unbelievable bad luck that the ball bounced back off someone's foot and ran him out. And yet half an hour later there he was talking airily of 'getting what he deserved'. Naturally there are exceptions that prove – as in 'test' – the rule, but they don't interest me. What matters is the average. What matters is the accumulation.

Time is the essence of this. Over time it evens out. Over time justice is done. Test batsmen know it. Over time their batting average is a very reliable indication of how good they were. They say that a career Test average of 40 is the bench-mark for a top-class player. I wouldn't know. Perhaps it is.

Personally I'm happy with anything over fifteen. But what I am confident about is that if you have an average of 40, you deserve it. And if your average is 38 – well, you deserve that too. No matter how many unlucky LBW decisions went against you. No matter how many times your bump ball was treated as a legitimate catch. No matter how many times you were run out through no fault of your own. The averages don't lie.

As I write there's an England batsman struggling with his form. Some voices call for his dismissal. Send him back to the counties. Let him rediscover himself there. Others say, no, he is a class act. You don't lose that ability. What you lose is your confidence in your ability. Let him stay. Let him play himself back into form. There are other attributes he brings to the team. What's the right choice? Who can say? There are other batsmen – perhaps equally as good – clamouring for his place. Should they not have the opportunity to show their mettle? Should they not be given the chance? What's that you say? They've already had their chance. They were selected and found wanting. Not once, but twice or more times. The averages don't lie. The batsman who has lost his form still has an average well above 40. The ones who would take his place do not. It's as simple as that. Ask the spread-betting firms. They know the odds.

As I write, Michael Vaughan's Test average is 42.9. Every time he goes in you can buy or sell him at the bookies for a margin around that figure. Sell at 38, buy at 48. Maybe there are some that will give you a better – narrower – spread. The spread betters know what they're doing because the averages don't lie. When Vaughan goes in you can reasonably expect him to make 42 or 43. Anything more than that and you're an optimist. Anything less than that and you're a pessimist. You can take other factors into account if you're a betting man. The quality of the opposition. The state of the pitch or the weather or his marriage. But over time, what's Vaughan going to make when he goes in to bat? Forty-three. Nothing he does now will do much to change his average. Perhaps he will have a disastrous run and it will fall below 40. I doubt it. Only if he makes ten ducks in a row, ten innings without a single run, will his average drop below 40. And that's not going to happen. He'll be dropped from the team before it gets that bad.[2]

Or perhaps he will make a hatful of runs this summer and it will rise. Perhaps – but again I doubt it. He's batted 141 times in Test matches, you see, and been out 132 times. To get his average to rise by one run in the next innings he must score 132 not out – or 175 if he is foolish enough to lose his wicket. And for another run? Do it again. And again? Like the string of ducks, it's not going to happen.

So that's who Michael Vaughan is. A wonderful batsman, an excellent captain and the man who brought us the Ashes in 2005. And a man with a batting average of 42.9. It was the same with Bradman. Bradman expected – was expected – to make a century every time he went into bat. But sometimes he made nought, just like the rest of us.

Is this true of everything else? I don't know. What I do know is that parenting is, like run scoring, an accumulation of a thousand small decisions. Our daughters are growing fast. Every day is a new adventure, every morning a new start. We don't ask ourselves if we are doing the right thing. We

[2] In fact, having secured a 2009 central contract, Michael Vaughan 'withdrew' from the England squad for the India tour at the end of 2008. His run of bad form meant it looked like he would be dropped anyway

simply do what we do and hope for the best. Perhaps what we are doing is right. Perhaps not. We have no choice but – in the cricketing phrase – to play each ball as it comes. In cricket the ball is in play when the bowler commences his delivery stride. But in that moment you have no idea what is coming. A benign half-volley just begging to be hit back over the bowler's head?

Or a steepling bouncer that skims your ears?

I LOVE…

Scoring off the edge

It is mid-morning when the boy wonder and my daughter descend from the heavens where they have no doubt been stargazing. She has an appointment to go shopping. There is a party at a friend's house and she needs a new frock. The boy dotes on her in almost every respect, but there are some depths to which he will not stoop. He will not, for example, go shopping. I regard this as a hopeful sign. A man who does not shop must fill his time by other means and was there ever something so perfectly designed to fill time as cricket?

But cricket's not on the agenda, although bonding is. The weather is showing signs of clearing and my daughter has a suggestion.

'Um, Da-ad,' she says.

'Ye-es?'

She purses her lips at my mimicry. The boy smiles into his fringe.

'Do we still have a video camera? A good one?'

'Ye-es…' We do. It's a good one. Left over from a shoot somewhere, back when I was a television producer. I must remember to give it back some day.

'Because you know he has sponsors?'

'He' is hovering in the background trying to pretend he's not hovering in the background. He is hopping from one foot to the other, as if he needs a pee. He is wearing regulation dress (jeans, sneakers with skulls on them, T-shirt, thin hoodie), remarkable only because his T-shirt has a slogan that reads 'Fighting for peace' (in BIG letters) 'is like fucking for virginity' (in very small letters). Below it is a graphic of something exploding, but I am not sure what. A bomb…? A…?

London 1997

There's an entry in my diary which needs no explanation. 1997 – so my daughter must have been all of six years old. 'There are definite signs of teenagerness about you,' I wrote. 'When I tripped on the stairs you looked down your nose at me. "Nice one, Dad," you said. I forgave you because I know I show signs of being a parent. So far (to my credit) I have managed to keep my lip buttoned about your appalling dress sense. I hereby swear to continue this silence up to but not including the moment when you have any body part pierced.'

Okay, so maybe it needs a little explanation. Her dress sense. It is not that it offends; it's just that it takes loyalty to extremes. And we are against extremes. We like the middle of the road. It's a nice place, with views on all sides. 'You have a pair of leggings which you insist on wearing. They are dark green and have a big (and growing) hole on the left knee. Every so often I make a feeble effort to spirit them out of your room and into the bin, but each time they miraculously reappear. Today was such a day. It was also sunny and I noticed that your left knee is slightly suntanned.'

And now, in the presence of the boy, her clothing is drifting goth-wards. Black on black. Stud on stud. Can it be long before the wretched question of body-piercing raises its head?

'Sorry, what was that?' I say. 'I lost concentration for a minute.' What *is* that thing on his T-shirt?

'But a lot of the footage of him is, like, not great,' says my daughter. (Mistress of understatement that she is. All of the footage of him on his skateboard is 'not great' and most of it is dreadful.) 'And so his sponsors were saying they need better and I was wondering if maybe you...'

'If?'

'If you would, you know, film him. Skateboarding.'

'What, now?'

'Are you busy?'

I wasn't busy. There was no cricket that day.

'Sure,' I say. 'Be happy to.' Maybe if he owes me he'll pay more attention to my cricket. My willingness takes them by surprise. For a moment you can see them wondering if they have made a big mistake. My daughter contemplates a few codicils, but she disguises them as terms-for-my-own-protection.

'You don't have to stay the whole time,' she says. 'Just do a little bit and then you can go.' Meaning, I can take all the kit back and he will stay and enjoy himself. 'It shouldn't take long.' And just to be sure. 'You'll be finished before lunch.'

'Sure,' I say. 'No problem.'

'And then you can go.' Meaning, must go.

'Sure.'

'Okay, um, excellent,' she says. 'I'll see you later.'

'Yeah, alright,' says her boy. I decide I had better take a cricket ball, just in case.

London 1993

We read *A Child's Garden of Verses* by Robert Louis Stevenson. I can quote most of them by heart. My daughter likes, 'Where Go The Boats?', which is the one about the dark brown river and the boats floating on the foam. She calls it her 'Dark Brown Poem' and she cries at the thought of 'other little children' taking the narrator's boats ashore.

'But why?' she asks. 'They're his boats.'

'Because they've sailed down the river. They've gone and he's left behind.'

'Is he happy?' she asks.

'I think so,' I say. 'He knows that the boats will find a home somewhere else.'

'He's very nice to share his boats,' she says.

'Well, sometimes in life you have to let things go. And it's okay because the boats will be looked after. They're not going to get hurt or anything. They're just going on a journey.'

She retreats to the land of counterpane, which doesn't go anywhere.

London 2007

I take her little boat ashore in Westminster Square. Too small for cricket but – apparently – perfect for skateboarding. Over the years many people have made the transition from field to front bench. Alfred Lyttelton was a fine batsman and wicket keeper who entered parliament and became Colonial Secretary under the watchful eye of his brother-in-law, Arthur Balfour. Alec Douglas-Home was another who played first-class cricket. The square is sandwiched between Methodist

Central Hall, Westminster Abbey, the Queen Elizabeth Conference Centre and the Palace of Westminster. Oh, and about 8,000 cars a minute hooting and tooting their way to Whitehall or Victoria or the Embankment or (the lucky ones) escaping south of the river where there is less traffic. The grass itself is relatively free of people; we have only Mandela, Churchill, Jan Smuts, a lady feeding the pigeons, three Japanese tourists and Brian Haw, the peace campaigner, for company.

'Why here?' I ask.

Because at the western edge of the square there is a paved section. And because leading on to the paved section are a series of low flat stairs. And because it is possible for skateboarders to speed along the upper paved section, bounce themselves on to the ledge alongside the stairs (being all the while careful to avoid the flowerpots) and 'grind' their way to the end where, all being well, they will land gracefully and do a circular swoop for the cameras. The place has the advantage also that the sound of the skateboards is drowned by the sound of traffic and that there is grass beyond the paving so that if things get out of control, there is a reasonable chance, say 50-50, of a soft landing.

Excellent. We get to work. The boy wonder has two mates, Mutty and Dogboy. Dogboy is the tall one with a stud in his left ear. Mutty is the short one with red trainers. Other than that I know nothing about them. Neither of them looks like a cricketer. The boy wonder is better at skateboarding than his mates and he takes it seriously. He does a couple of trial runs. He experiments with various settings on his wheels. He plans what he is going to do. It all looks a bit prissy to me. Can't he just get on with it? But I know that I must, under no circumstances, say anything. I am merely there to film.

And, by osmosis, this will count as bonding. Because he'll owe me.

So I concentrate on setting up the camera. I work methodically. He does a run and I film it in wide shot. I grab a couple of cutaways. A pigeon chooses that moment to empty its bowel on Churchill's head. Also excellent. A little comedy to leaven the skateboarding. I get a shot of Mandela as well, but I've always found that sculpture a little unsatisfying. It is not quite in proportion. His body is too small for his head and that, together with his stance, gives the whole thing a slight feeling of Charlie Chaplin. Of whom I'm a fan, you understand, just not in the same way. Then we confer. I explain the sequence I have in mind. Wide shot as he throws the board down and runs for it, close up of foot hitting board, close of spinning wheels, POV of board hurtling to steps, close as he presses down on the springs to create the uplift… and so on. He's impressed I can tell and doesn't even mind that he will have to do it eight or nine times for me to get all the shots. His mates are impressed too.

'He's a pro, you know,' says Mutty to Dogboy. I pretend not to hear. 'He's in the industry.' Not true, but we'll let it go. I was once and that's got to count for something. Mutty has ambitions to work as a sound recordist. Every now and then he comes over and lightly runs his hands over the windsock I have mounted on the camera mike. I know I should offer him the opportunity to put it on the boom, but to be honest that's too much like hard work. He'd only get the damn thing in shot the whole time.

Meanwhile the boy wonder is going through the routine over and over. Each time he attempts it he gets a little better. His bounce is higher. His grind is more controlled. His landing is more graceful. He's beginning to put little flourishes in. He holds his hand just so as he grinds, like he's holding a tea cup at the Ritz. He straightens his body, the way skiers will when they have mastered a slope. He starts to remove his hoodie and when I shake my head he nods and says, 'Continuity?'

Like the old pro he is. One day he'll be 'in the industry'.

And after about half an hour of this we have most of the sequence.

'Excellent,' I say. 'Perfect. You should be on TV.'

His face clouds. 'I thought...?'

I have to explain I'm only joking. I had been filming it. He is – or will be – on his version of TV. It's in the can. It happened. But it was also boring. All that stopping and starting. All me yelling at him when to go and when to wait. You can hear it on the rushes. 'Not yet, not yet... okay, go... Sorry, we're going to have to do that again. I missed the focus pull.' So they're happy to take a break.

Me too. Even though it is well known that in cricket, if you really want to get someone out, someone who has been in for a long time, the best thing to do is have a drinks break. It always affects the batsmen more than the fielders. The bowlers feel rejuvenated; the batsmen feel disconcerted. They have to allow some time to play themselves back in. But often they don't. Ask Strauss or Pietersen or any of the other English batsmen who got themselves out soon after lunch or tea or the drinks break in the summer of 2007. It happened so regularly it was almost predictable. For different reasons, mind you. Strauss because he is not in great touch. Pietersen because he was trying to prove what great touch he is in.

Time to wrap up. 'Okay,' I say, 'we're pretty much done. In the bag. It'll make a nice sequence. But before I go we need one more shot of you.' Not strictly true. We didn't need it. I already had the shot. But then again it could be better. Why not try and get it one more time.

Which just goes to show that perfection is overrated. Be happy with what you've got. It wasn't that he did anything wrong or different. It was a trick – a 180 ollie off the front edge of a wall lining the stairs – he had done several times before. So I asked him to do it one more time. For the cameras. For posterity. For me.

He was happy to oblige.

What went wrong? I don't know. Perhaps his timing was off. Perhaps he hit a pebble. Perhaps there was a gust of wind. Perhaps a butterfly waved its wings in Peru. Whatever the cause, the outcome was clear. He missed his footing on landing. His ankle twisted and then broke. His board went shooting off straight at me. I skipped to get out of the way, lost my footing and swooped up in the air. When I came down my keys had buried themselves three inches deep in my, well, meaty shank.

I screamed, he yelled (it may have been the other way round) and when the dust had settled, Mutty and Dogboy headed for home while the boy wonder and I found a cab to take us across the river to the A&E department at St Thomas's Hospital. They treated me first. There were a couple of male nurses in casualty that day and much joking about what prison warders refer to as an 'incident in the exercise yard' as they used tongs to remove my car keys from my backside. But the wound was too messy for stitches. They cleaned it up, slapped on a plaster and suggested I might like to think about growing up.

London 1994

Our children take shape in ways we hardly recognise. What starts as an undifferentiated blob of joy evolves into something more substantial. Something more recognisable. Something more mobile. Corners appear and quirks. There will be accommodations to be made. I know this. All the books tell us so. But for the moment we see none of it; we see only my daughter and her ready smile. At the nursery she attends, the manager uses her to attract other parents. Forgetting I'm her father, she points my daughter out to me. 'This one is always smiling,' she says. At home too. Her gurgle fills the hallway. Her splashes cover the wall.

My girlfriend has been in New York for some days; our daughter is one and a bit. She recognises both my girlfriend and her absence. There is a large photograph of her on the wall and each time my daughter passes it she pauses to point and say 'Mummy', in much the same way as Catholics in a hurry will half-genuflect before getting on with the business of the day.

My girlfriend calls us from a booth on the corner of 53rd and 5th. It is some crazy hour of the morning. Like the Joan Baez song, only not in the midWest.

'Well, I'll be damned,' I quote. 'There comes your voice again.'

'I just wanted to say hello,' she says on cue.

Me too, but our daughter is having none of it. She sits up in bed, pulls the phone from my grasp and looks at it intently. Then she holds it up to her head, like she has seen me do. Only she gets it the wrong way round. She gurgles into the earpiece. She 'talks where she should listen and listens where she should talk'.

Substitute 'when' for 'where' and it's a pretty good description of her now.

In the waiting room for X-rays, the boy was looking a bit pale. The second wave of pain, the one that hits after the body has done its shock therapy, was kicking in.

'Is she here yet?' he asked.

She soon was. She had hot-footed it (as hotly as a London bus will let you foot it) from her shopping appointment and arrived breathless and concerned to find me, but not him.

'Where is he?' she asked.

'Getting X-rayed.'

'What have you done to him?'

The presumption of parental guilt is, of course, well established in English law. You have only to read the newspapers on any given day to realise that whatever anybody does – not even young people, any people – we blame the parents. Primarily the mother. A child goes on the rampage? The mother's fault. A group of yobs tear down a house? Mothers. Teenage drinkers? The mother. Teenage mothers? The mother. And, no, I don't mean the teenager. I mean her mother. Even if she became a mother when she was a teenager.

But in the absence of a mother, the father will do.

'I have done nothing,' I said, *'save devote my skills to the pursuit of his dreams.'*

Actually I didn't say that. I could see her distress was real. I could see that her whole long summer of love was now under threat. There is, somewhere in the bowels of English culture, an alternative summer to the one the toffs experience. For them it is all laid out. May Ball... Lord's... Wimbledon... Ascot... Glyndebourne... Cheltenham. For north London teenagers, the roll call is the same only different. Reading,

Glastonbury, Leeds, V, T in the Park and so on. One long summer of music and... well, whatever else came with the music. I shall give her credit. Let's say she had been looking forward to a long summer of music and love in the company of the boy wonder.

Until this.

I almost feel sorry for her.

His X-rays come back. It isn't serious, but it is broken. A metatarsal. Don't know which one. Don't much care. Five weeks in plaster and a few more after that on crutches. By which time summer will be nearly over.

'What are we going to do?' says my daughter. 'He can't get around like that. Think of the mud.'

It was hard not to think of the mud. In the public mind Glastonbury is associated entirely with mud. And for good reason.

'We can hang out,' he says. Meaning in her room, the one where she has a big soft double bed.

'I suppose,' says my daughter. I sense a glimmer of hope.

'And we can travel by bus.'

'What, with crutches?'

Kilimanjaro, you see. Since we had done all that training a few years before, she had become a determined walker. Her daily trip to school was a good half-hour walk each way. Oxford Street is only 55 minutes' walk from our house. Buses had become an option of last resort. Even free ones, 'like wot Ken had given us'.

'Dad,' she says, returning to an earlier theme. 'This is all your fault. If you hadn't insisted on filming him...'

We'll leave the injustice aside – because I had a suggestion.

'I know the perfect thing to do with a broken leg,' I say.

Oh yes?

'We could go to Lord's,' I say, 'to watch the cricket.'

'Thanks, but no thanks,' says my daughter.

'Oh,' says her boy.

'No,' says my daughter.

She held the boy's hand and squeezed it. She looked deep into his eyes. She pushed aside his fringe and made sure he was looking into hers. Who knows what promises were exchanged in that look? And slowly she shook her head. I thought of Annie. I thought of my promises not to talk about cricket. I thought of the summer breeze in the sugar cane. I thought of the stars at night and of the way young people will, eventually and despite their parents, roll all their strength and all their sweetness into one ball. I thought of red nails on whisky glasses.

Perhaps his pain was greater than we thought.

'No,' says my daughter.

'Actually,' says her true love, 'that would be cool.'

Edged past the keeper for four, and nothing she or the slips could do about it.

I LOVE …

Umpires

The court of final appeal, also known as the Highest Court in the Land, is in session, accompanied by the smell of macaroni cheese cooking and Nanci Griffith on the radio.

'You're kidding?' says the Lord Chief Justice, also known as my girlfriend. A question.

'You're kidding!' says my daughter. Counsel for the prosecution. Half an accusation; half a plea.

Then she changes her mind.

'Mum, talk to him? He's not kidding.'

'Why?' says my girlfriend.

To me, you understand, not to my daughter.

'I thought it would be nice,' I say. I am the defendant. 'It'll be fun.'

My girlfriend has a strong instinct for natural justice. Her and Nanci. Nanci is singing that old Woodie Guthrie song, the one about the Okies who trek across to California only to find that it ain't no paradise, not unless you've got that *do-re-mi*. A bit like Lord's then. Lord's is the most perfect place on earth – as long as you've got that *do-re-mi*.

'What did he say?' she asks.

'He said yes. He said it would be cool.'

'He said "might". Not would. Might. He didn't know what he was saying,' says my daughter.

Actually he said 'would', but I let it pass.

'His foot was broken. He was in pain,' she continues. 'God knows what drugs they had given him.' As an afterthought she adds, 'You broke it. You probably did it on purpose.'

I would have said 'objection, your honour', but my girlfriend is still working on getting the parameters straight.

'You're going to go for the whole day?' she asks.

'Sure.'

'But that's how long?'

'Six hours.'

'It's more,' says my daughter. 'They have lunch.'

She makes it sound slightly worse than genocide.

'And they buy stuff.'

'Oh, God,' says my girlfriend. 'Shopping for boys.' Yes, well, okay, I admit I sometimes buy cricket junk. Not replica kits, I hasten to add. I have never bought a replica kit. Except once. My son and I went to Paris for the 2007 Rugby World Cup final and for a joke I wore a Springbok jersey while my son wore an English one. We didn't have tickets, mind you. Like thousands of others we were camped under the Eiffel Tower and watched the match on the big screen. But the (almost entirely English) crowd were not in the mood for irony and became unpleasantly aggressive about my split loyalties (actually not split at all; I was supporting England all the way) and eventually I covered up the South African jersey. But I do like other stuff. I like cricket books and those miniature balls they sell. They have a comforting, Captain Queeg quality about them. And I like miniature bats with poor-quality reproduction pictures of cricket players. I have one with Mike Atherton's autograph. I got it at Lord's during the terribly mismatched Test against Zimbabwe in 2000. The Zimbabweans were all out for 83 in the first innings. A ridiculous score for a Test match. Hardly a match at all and certainly not a test. We went on the third day and saw both Hick and Stewart get centuries as England built up an unassailable lead on their way to an easy victory.

'It's for my son,' I said when Atherton signed it.

'They always are,' he replied. Next time I'll say it's for my daughter.

Back home the court is still in session in the kitchen. Nanci is going on about the fairground ride, 'the wall of death'. A Richard Thompson song. The 'wall of death' is the nearest she gets to being alive. She should try skateboarding.

'He's gone?' says my girlfriend. She means the boy wonder. I nod. He had disappeared back home, complete with his broken foot and lipstick on his collar. I had to avert my eyes while he and my daughter said goodbye. The plan was that he would reappear come Thursday. To go to Lord's with me. Unless my daughter, his true love, succeeds in her attempt to petition the Highest Court in the Land to see whether she could get the decision made in the A&E of St Thomas's Hospital reversed.

The Highest Court in the Land remains inscrutable.

'Why?' she says.

'I thought it would be fun. I mean, Lord's is special. It's a place every boy should go and he's never been. Or girl,' I add with a meaningful look at my daughter.

She puts out a tongue. She will be at school. Not that she would come anyway. She came to one match once, in 1999, to see the Black Caps win their first ever Test at Lord's after a fairly dismal display from England. And she was so bored and so restless we left soon after lunch.

'It's part of the English landscape,' I say. 'There are millions and millions of people who have been to Lord's and each of them has special memories of the place. It's like nowhere else on earth.'

I'm quoting virtually everyone involved in cricket. Take a stroll around the Lord's ground and you see it written everywhere. Past and present stars of the international game are all quoted saying just how much Lord's means to them. And they're right. It is the home of cricket and somehow it manages still to embody the better parts of the game. The ground is named for the man who originally leased the land, Thomas Lord, but its heart was always partly with the eponymous nobility. As the official MCC history puts it, 'Aristocrats and noblemen played their cricket in White Conduit Fields at Islington, London. Like shooting and fox-hunting, cricket was considered a manly sport for the elite – with plenty of gambling opportunities to boot. (Around £20,000 was bet on a series of games between Old Etonians and England in 1751!)

'As London's population grew, so did the nobility's impatience with the crowds who gathered to watch them play. In pursuit of exclusivity, they decided to approach Thomas Lord, a bowler with White Conduit CC, and asked him to set up a new private ground.'

Lord was a businessman. He leased land at what is now Dorset Square and the Marylebone Cricket Club was established. Lord promoted his first match – between Kent and Sussex – there in 1787. The lease expired and after a short stay in what is now Regent's Park, the MCC and Lord's moved to the current location (formerly a duck pond) in St

John's Wood in 1814. So perhaps we shouldn't worry about the Indian Premier Leagure or about Sir Clive Stanford and his millions. The game has always had its boosters.

And now back to the action:

'And anyway you were the one who said I should spend time with him,' I say to my beloved. 'You were the one who said I should try to bond with him.'

(Note to would-be barristers: In my limited experience, trying to turn the trial judge into one of the accused is a high-risk strategy and 99 times out of 100 it will fail. It's like winning the toss in cricket. You can choose to do whatever you like as long as you bat. Even when the conditions clearly favour the bowlers, when the pitch is soggy, the wind is blowing and the air is heavy with damp. Then you may for a moment think about choosing to field. And then you bat. So it is when you go to trial. You think about accusing the judge of all sorts of things – and then you don't. It's not worth it.)

'Mum!' says my daughter. She's genuinely horrified. 'You didn't? What were you thinking?'

The Highest Court in the Land is unfamiliar with the Bradman Card Manoeuvre. I have never shared that particular memory with her. I'm not sure what she would read into it. She would be suspicious of the star story. She would query the accuracy of my recollection of the conversation. She would almost certainly impugn my morals on the is-that-all-you-lot-ever-think-about grounds. And then she would no doubt look smugly down her nose at me. The cat that got the cream. Our own seduction (this is the part I was reluctant to discuss with my daughter when she asked had I, like, known my girlfriend was the one) had occurred during a brief break in proceedings at a political rally. There were no fathers in attendance and no mention was made of cricket. Nor was it necessary for me to talk about the stars. Or for her to tell me she liked it. Our own seduction was essentially pragmatic.

But that's another story. The HCITL moves swiftly on.

'What's in it for you?' she asks.

I have to restrain myself from calling her 'your honour'.

'Nothing,' I say. Same as marriage.

She looks like she believes me. There is nothing in it for me.

'Except the cricket?' she said. We'll pretend it's a question. Actually it was an accusation.

'Except the cricket,' I agree. Guilty as charged.

My daughter sensed this one was slipping away.

'What will I do?' she asks. Plaintively.

'You'll be at school,' I say. 'You won't even notice we're gone.'

'We finish at three. When does the cricket end?'

'Six…'

'Meaning seven,' says my daughter. 'Only yesterday you told me they never finish on time. You said they take as long as they bloody like. You said the whatever they're called, the people who run the thing? You said they should be more strict.'

Which is true. I had said that. The people who run the thing, whatever they're called, should be more strict. They should ensure that the paying customers get their full 90 overs in the day.

'And so you'll only leave there at seven. And be back here by eight. And then he's going home.'

Which is also true.

'It's not like I get to see him often.'

Which is a matter of opinion. Since the boy wonder had first graced our doorstep a few weeks before, he had settled into a pattern of coming 'round' twice a week. And longer at weekends. Saturday morning to Sunday afternoon. For the Lord's visit the timetable was to be changed slightly. He would come 'round' on the Thursday. His school had what they now call an Inset day and what older hands amongst us know as a Baker day, meaning a day when the teachers get in-service training and the kids roam the streets in feral bands terrorising pensioners and knocking over newsagents. Her school did not. And on the Friday – the joys of A-levels – he didn't have to be at his school at all. He did, however, have to attend a family event on the Saturday. So the deal was struck. He would come over early on Thursday. Together we would go to Lord's. My daughter would go to school. And some time in the evening they would be reunited for a decorous dinner. And on Friday she would be in school again. Time was he would have spent the morning skateboarding and then appeared at her school gate to escort her home. But with his broken foot this was no longer an option.

'Mu-um?' says my daughter. Her version of closing argument. The cases had been made. It was time for the Highest Court in the Land to give its view.

'Think of it this way,' says the HCITL. 'It'll put him off for life.'

My daughter has a naturally sunny disposition. She is prepared to assume the best about virtually everything.

Except possibly me.

'But what if it doesn't?' she says.

'Tell him no sex,' says my girlfriend. The pragmatic one, remember.

'Mum!' says my daughter. 'How can you say that?'

Good question. It was all I could do not to smile. I may have been wrong, but I was sure that in that cry I heard the plaintive tones of one for whom the withholding of favours was not yet an option. You have to give them before you can withhold them. In that sense anyway.

'That goes for you too,' my girlfriend said. Meaning me.

'Yes, your honour.'

It's a cricket thing, you see. This absolute respect for the umpire. Actually there's a case for saying it's not. Recently the ICC has, in its wisdom, decided to change the result of a match that happened two years ago. It was England v. Pakistan at the Oval in 2006. After a row about ball-tampering, Pakistan were held to have defaulted by refusing to return to the field of play after tea. And so they lost the match. But now the ICC has decided there were 'special circumstances' (i.e. the umpires blew it) and the match was in fact drawn. Incredible but true. And a very poor precedent. But we hope that is the exception. In general the spirit of cricket requires maximum respect for the umpire. The laws demand it. And the game doesn't work without it. Mostly this relates to getting out. There are ten ways of getting out in cricket. If you caught me in a good mood early in the morning I could probably recite them all. Only one of them – bowled – doesn't really need a decision from the umpire. But the rules – sorry, *laws*; cricket doesn't have rules – are clear. A batsman may only be given out on appeal. The umpire cannot send the batsman back to the pavilion unless the fielding side has asked him to do so. This is the 'appeal'. And – on appeal – it is left to the umpire to decide whether a batsman is out. In the kind of matches in which I play this puts the umpire in an invidious position, because he is one of the opposing team (unless I have been promoted beyond my station in which case we have 'official officials' who are paid to be there) and is therefore being asked to give one of his teammates out. Umpires are most commonly called to give judgement on appeals for leg before wicket. It's often said that the LBW law is complicated. This is not so. The LBW law says:

> The striker is out LBW in the circumstances set out below.
> (a) The bowler delivers a ball, not being a no ball
> and (b) the ball, if it is not intercepted full pitch, pitches in line between wicket and wicket or on the off side of the striker's wicket
> and (c) the ball not having previously touched his bat, the striker intercepts the ball, either full pitch or after pitching, with any part of his person
> and (d) the point of impact, even if above the level of the bails either (i) is between wicket and wicket or (ii) is either between wicket and wicket or outside the line of the off stump, if the striker has made no genuine attempt to play the ball with his bat
> and (e) but for the interception, the ball would have hit the wicket.

The difficult part for the umpire is not understanding the law, but applying it. Where did the ball pitch? Did it hit the pad first? Would it have hit the stumps? And the answer to all of these is: *it doesn't really matter.* What matters is what the umpire decides. If he says you're out – you're out. If not, then not. Think of Mike Atherton at Trent Bridge against Allan Donald in 1998. One the most delicious – is that the word? – periods of play seen in modern Test cricket started when a Donald ball clipped Atherton on the glove and ballooned to Boucher behind the stumps. Atherton didn't walk. Umpire Dunne didn't give him out and for the next half an hour or so Donald bowled as hard and fast and murderously as anyone, ever. And Atherton withstood it. It was, he says, 'the most intense period of cricket' he had ever experienced. For me too and I was only listening on the radio. I can't begin to imagine what it was like to play it. And it all started because the umpire said not out. Atherton says Donald called him a 'fucking cheat', but later they shared a beer and – nice touch – Atherton presented Donald with the offending glove.

In our kitchen the Highest Court in the Land said 'not out'.

On the Wednesday my daughter made one more attempt.

'You'll be bored,' she said into the phone. The sofa has moulded itself around her habitual phone position. She's lying on her back with one leg on the sofa arm and the other on the floor. Her head is hanging off the edge of the seat and her newly black hair trails on the floor. I think she likes it because it lets her hair hang down and she can play with it while she talks. She winds it in her fingers. She places it on top of her head and watches it fall, a soft avalanche across her peaches-and-cream complexion. You can trace her story through her hair. Its styles, its colours. The reply was obviously unsatisfactory.

'He'll understand,' she said. 'He knows you're only doing it to please him.'

She had already tried a couple of gambits. The 'but what about what I want?' tactic didn't seem to have had much effect. Easily rebuffed, I guessed, with a swift, 'It's only one day.' And the threat of being with me didn't seem to work either. I couldn't hear the other end of the conversation, so you'll have to fill in the missing words yourself.

'No, he's not,' she said. 'He's boring.'

That didn't work either.

'Well, you'll be bored. Because nothing happens.'

He must have asked how she knew.

'Dad told me,' she said.

I LOVE . . .

The gaps between balls

'I told you,' says my girlfriend.

Yes, well.

'You should have kept your mouth shut.'

I know.

'But you didn't.'

No.

'There'll be a price to pay.'

Yes, alright, thank you. I get the picture. And I know there will be a price to pay. I just don't, yet, know what it is. And I know I should have kept my mouth shut – except my daughter would have known anyway that for most of the time in cricket, nothing happens. It's an old complaint and part of me concedes that she has a point. Let us for the moment confine ourselves to Test cricket. Play takes place over five days for six hours a day. In fact each 'day' takes a little longer than six hours because Test cricketers are inclined to do things at their own pace, which is somewhat slower than the approved pace. But for the sake of argument let's agree that in each six-hour, 360-minute, 21,600-second day a total of 90 overs – 540 balls – will be bowled.

That's 40 seconds per ball, which is roughly eight times

what is required. The length of a cricket pitch is 66 feet. The distance from the moment the bowler releases the ball to the moment the batsman hits it (or lets it go by to the wicket keeper) is somewhat less. Perhaps 56 feet. Spin bowlers bowl at about 55 mph. Fast bowlers bowl at around 85 mph. There is less than half a second from the moment the bowler begins his 'delivery stride' (at which point the ball is 'in play') to the moment the batsman hits the ball. A ball hit for four will usually reach the boundary in less than three seconds. A ball which is hit but does not reach the boundary will be returned to the wicket keeper (at which point the ball is 'dead') in less than five seconds. Half of all balls bowled are ignored and are dead the moment the wicket keeper catches them. On average, each ball is in play for three seconds. That leaves 37 seconds when nothing happens. Five hundred and forty times a day, for 37 seconds at a time, nothing happens. That's 19,980 seconds or 333 minutes. Over the course of a five-day match, the ball is dead for nearly 28 hours.

And when the ball is dead, nothing, by definition, happens.

'Hello,' I say.

'Yeah, alright,' he replies.

The ball goes dead.

No, okay, that's not entirely fair. Things happen, but not so you would notice. On the Thursday he arrives at the appointed hour. Too late for my daughter who, in a fit of high dudgeon, has had to leave for school before he knocks on the door.

'Just be nice, okay?' she says as she leaves. 'Don't try to teach him anything.'

One of those tricky promises, but I make it anyway. There's a get-out in the semantics. I won't *try* to teach him anything.

My teaching will be effortless. Like my cricket. Like my lofted shots to but not quite over the man at mid-wicket.

He's not dressed up for the occasion. The T-shirt, the one about fighting for peace, has been replaced by a death's head on a motorcycle, but otherwise he looks the same. Except, somehow different. At first I can't place it. There's something new. He looks somehow taller. Stronger. More upright. And then I realise what it is. He's cut his hair back a little. He no longer has to lean to one side to peer beneath it. He joins me in the kitchen where I am packing my only mildly obsessive Test-match-watching kit: radio, umbrella, binoculars, pen, crossword collection and as much cash as I can lay my hands on. For food and incidentals. Like miniature bats. Or balls. Or brightly packaged goods in the Lord's shop.

'Binoculars?' he asks.

It's a big field. From side on it is very hard to see the ball when it's bowled at 90 mph. I remember the first time I went to Lord's. There must have been twenty overs gone before my eyes adjusted sufficiently for me to see the balls being rained down by the West Indian trio of Garner, Small and Marshall.

Umbrella?

Obvious. 'Have you got one?'

He hasn't. We find an old one in the cellar.

Crosswords? No explanation needed. My daughter has long since explained to him my other odd addiction. Secretly he's relieved. The more I have to do, the less he has to talk.

'I could teach you,' I say.

'Um,' he replies.

We look at the rest of the kit.

'And the radio?'

Of all the items in my kit, the radio is most important. Why? See 'binoculars' above. It's a big field and you won't really be able to keep up with everything that's happening unless you are in touch with the *Test Match Special* team at all times. Because, contrary to my daughter's mathematics about 'nothing happening', you have only to listen to the *Test Match Special* radio commentary on the BBC to know that there is lots going on. Lots to talk about. Plenty of things of interest. Especially for Jonathan Agnew, who has the endearing ability to be interested in almost anything. Not least the pretty brunette in the sunhat in block B. Or the gentleman in the MCC tie looking tired and emotional (and out of place; why is he not in the Pavilion?) in the Compton Stand. Or the latest machinations of the money men who, as I write, are fighting for the soul of cricket. Actually not the soul. I suspect that none of them give a fig for the soul of cricket. What they care about is the beautiful virtuous equation that says cricket = television = money = more cricket = more television = more money. It has always been this way. Cricket has its roots in gaming and what is the point of gaming if not for the money men to make more money? The IPL and Sir Allen Stanford are only the latest in a very, very long line of men. The distinction between 'professional' and 'amateur' was dropped in 1962 – henceforth all players were to be known 'simply as cricketers' – but money had been a factor in the game long before that.

It doesn't matter. Aggers will talk to them all. And then segue seamlessly to the pigeons on the Grand Stand roof. Or the reason why this rock star or that opera singer is devoted to cricket. Or the scudding rain. Or the unexpected arrival of royalty at a match. During the Trent Bridge Test against New Zealand in 2008, Aggers was very interested in the impending arrival of the Duke of Edinburgh at his local airfield, the one from which he pilots his own aircraft. Listening to *TMS* is like having a direct link to the inner workings of Middle England's Middle-Aged Middlemen. They talk about the weather and batting averages, about tactics, clouds and the many shades of green to be found in a cricket field. The Inuit and their supposed plethora of words for snow are no contest for an Englishman and his lawn. Our *TMS* team eat chocolate cake. They get the giggles. They use – and reuse – the same adjectives. Sumptuous (if the batsman is Australian) or abject (if he's English). Aggressive (South African) or volatile (Indian). Spirited (Sri Lankan) or naïve (West Indian). They chat about old times. They tease Bill, the scorer. They say their piece – and move on. The producers insist they do it in stints of only twenty minutes each because they know that if the commentators stay longer, they will go mad or – which is worse – run out of things to say. The pair taking over then say everything the departing pair just said, pausing only to add, from time to time, that 'the ball goes through to the keeper and there's no run there'.

And anyway (he said defensively), even when the ball is dead, the men of *TMS* are right. There is always something going on. Cricket has evolved a substantial vocabulary to deal with it. The batsmen might indulge in a spot of gardening. Short leg might drop backward of square. Deep extra cover might slot into the gully. Silly mid-off might come to his senses. From time to time the captain will ask mid-on to give him ten or suggest that third slip take a position at deep mid-wicket, which (by the way) is the cricketing equivalent of suggesting to one's lover that she (or he) can sleep on the wet patch. The vice-captain will shine the ball on an area of his groin that seems to the casual observer to be suspiciously intimate. The wicket keeper will clap and applaud and talk about 'nice areas', whatever that means. The star batsman languishing at third man will take his Kookaburra polycarbonate Genesis pro-sportsman's sunglasses off – and put them on again. And the crowd will try to get a Mexican wave going.

'I like Mexican waves,' said her true love. 'They're cool.'

I know this because she told me.

'It's like he wasn't listening to a word I was saying,' she said. 'It was like he had already made up his mind to go with you.'

Ah, the pre-empt. I am also familiar with the pre-empt, whether in domestic matters or when batting. Pietersen's outrageous (How did he do it? I still can't quite understand how he got such power on the shot) reverse sweep was premeditated. He had decided long before Muralitharan let go of the ball what he was going to do and then he did it to outrageous effect. But just as often – in fact *more* often – the pre-empt ties the batsman up in knots. The bowler sees it coming and changes his approach. Instead of looping it up on off stump he spears it low and quick at leg stump. The batsman, who was thinking of reverse-sweeping, finds himself playing a defensive prod with the bat the wrong way up. And so on. Premeditated shots sometimes work. But sometimes they don't. It is the same in domestic matters. 'I've said I'll play tonight,' I say on the e-mail to my one true love. 'Sorry about that. Crisis. Last-minute thing. Twenty20 game. They were one short. Should be done by nine. Hope it's okay for you to do the shopping, pick up the kids, fix the leaking gutter, cook dinner for the four guests I had forgotten we had and while you're at it would you mind sending my mum her birthday present and fixing the hole in my other pair of whites because I've also agreed to play on Saturday.'

All of which only makes sense if the pre-empt is irreversible.

'What's in it for me?' says my true love. I'm paraphrasing, but that was the gist of it.

To which I shrug my shoulders (only she can't see that because I am sheltering behind the safety wall of the e-mail).

'Sorry, but I've committed now. I can't let the team down.'

Well, actually, yes I can. People do it all the time – and sometimes because they realise their love lives are in jeopardy. They don't admit it, of course. They maintain they have had to pull out at the last minute because their firm has sent them to explore the South Pole or because they have a thigh strain or because they have recently converted to a particularly restrictive form of pagan worship in which cows, the source of leather cricket balls, form the centrepiece. But what they really mean is that their loved one has thrown a strop and threatened to throw them out of the house if they go and spend one more day playing that bloody game (with those bloody people) and they have decided that in this case discretion is the better part of divorce.

But, assuming that one's relationship does not resemble the Norfolk coast and is not about to be washed away in the next big tidal surge, the pre-empt can sometimes work.

'Oh, well, if it's for the team, of course you can play,' says my loved one. Only she doesn't quite put it like that either.

So there we are on the first morning of the first Test match of the summer of 2007. Packed and ready to go. Eager to bond. On crutches. And me with a sore butt.

'You looking forward to this?' I ask.

Tempting fate, I know, but I can't resist. Maybe it's my fault, maybe not. I have allowed myself to get excited. Now I could plead innocence and say that I always look forward to the first day of the first Test. The soft hum of the crowd. The buzz of anticipation. The blank scorecards. The unnatural sparkle of the grass in May. The fresh breeze that should help bowlers coming up the slope from the Nursery End. But the fact is I am pleased to be going with him. We didn't exactly bond over the skateboarding outing, but nor was it an unmitigated disaster. Disaster, yes. But unmitigated, no. His little YouTube film, complete with music and graphics, is adjudged to have been a great success. He and his mates are well pleased. Mutty has pronounced me 'well cool'. But filming it hadn't been the breakthrough I was hoping for. It was just me shouting orders and him doing his thing. It's not like we talked. Or shared. Or anything-at-all-ed. He remains opaque to me. I don't know what (or whether) he thinks about anything. I don't know what he feels about my daughter. I don't know what he wants from life.

He shrugs.

'I guess.'

It seemed there was nothing else to say. Or perhaps he just didn't know how to say it.

I LOVE …

The 1984 West Indian team

He hugged me all the way there.

We were on my motorbike at the time, so this is not quite as intimate as it sounds. He had his crutches between us, like a latter-day standard bearer leading (or following?) the troops into battle. It was spitting rain and we were a little late and I took the speed bumps at slightly more than the approved speed. Each time we would go spiralling off into orbit and when we came to earth I could feel him readjust his position and mutter something to himself. Hail Mary, perhaps. But I love the motorbike. It is to London what oil is to an engine. It makes it all work. It makes it all easy. It removes stress and cost. It means you can guarantee journey times. And it removes contact with other people's armpits. Listen, for example, to Ben Dirs reporting for the BBC on that first day of the first Test at Lord's in the summer of 2007: 'Aaah, the English summer. The sound of leather on willow, the smell of freshly cut grass. Village folk dancing round the maypole, attractive ladies in strappy tops, aggressive-looking men with their shirts off drinking strong lager in town centres. Finding yourself nuzzling an unwashed armpit on the Tube in 50C heat.'

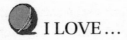

None of that for us. We have the wind in our faces (or as much wind as you can rustle up at 32.8 mph) and the anticipation of a day's cricket ahead.

There are really only two rules for riding pillion: hold tight, but not too tight, and do not try to steer. My daughter is a natural. Probably all that time she spent on the back of my bicycle when she was a kid. Sucking on a lolly and telling me to go faster while I pedalled my way up Highbury Hill. The boy is the same. He doesn't hold too tight. He barely holds at all. He rests his arms on me lightly, like a butterfly. To his credit he doesn't steer either. He has a natural feel for how to round corners. Novice riders will often lean backwards as the bike goes into a corner. The better thing is to lean forward. He does it instinctively like the skateboarder he is. I take a couple of speed bumps too fast, just to keep him interested, but he's getting used to it. Maybe he used to ride horses. I can feel him gripping with his knees and leaning into me. Nicely done.

We park in St John's Wood High Street, near the north gate to Lord's. I suppose if I had been thinking about it I would have made sure that we went in through the Grace Gates. The Grace Gates are the main entrance to the ground and are on the south side which, as it happens, is where we have seats. But I hadn't quite realised that this was a 'moment' for the boy. That this was a first and that he was looking forward to it. That it mattered to him. That he had always wanted to go, not to cricket, but to Lord's, which is not quite the same thing. Cricket is just cricket. Cricket at Lord's is – well, cricket at Lord's. The self-proclaimed home of cricket. The place where it all began. Actually not true – but true *enough*. Lord's is special. Lord's is imbued with the game's history. Lord's is wonderful.

The boy is nervous. He's looking around suspiciously, like a man walking down a dark alley. Wondering if the portly gentleman in the crinkled linen suit and MCC tie is going to mug him. Or ask him to pull his trousers up.

'Is there anything I should know?' he asks.

And suddenly I realise I am in a strange position. For all my adult life I have been an immigrant, an outsider. I have had England explained to me. Now I am the one in the know. This young man, in his death-metal T-shirt and skateboarder's shoes, with his floppy fringe and gentle smile – he feels like the outsider. This – Lord's more than cricket – is an England he doesn't know. And he is nervous.

'How do you mean?'

'You keep saying Lord's like it should mean something,' he says in a sudden display of insight. 'But I don't know what. I mean, I've never been here before. It's like you have this whole Lord's thing that I know nothing about.'

Oh.

Yes, I suppose I do. I should explain.

The first time I went to Lord's was in 1984.

'Before she was born?'

Yes, before 'she' was born. Before she was a twinkle in my eye. Before history began. And not long after I arrived in England from South Africa. To get here my girlfriend and I had hitchhiked across Africa. The first thing I did was buy the old motorbike. The second thing I did was go to Lord's. The memory of Lord's lasted longer than the motorbike. It packed up after a few months and I changed my allegiance to bicycles because pedalling kept me warm. It took me twenty years to work out that if you wanted to ride a motorbike you also had to buy warm clothes. Even in summer.

The cricket match was about a different allegiance altogether. It was the second Test against the West Indies in the 'blackwash' tour of that year. England had lost the first Test by an innings and 180 runs after the tourists put on a mammoth first innings total of 606 for four or five. And Andy Lloyd had been hit on the head by a Malcolm Marshall bouncer. He spent several days in hospital and never played Test cricket again. The second Test started better. All out for 286 in the first innings (Fowler made a century), England managed to get the great West Indian team out for 245. Viv Richards made 'only' 72. A win looked possible when, with the help of a grafting hundred from Allan Lamb, England made 300 for nine in the second innings. Ian (now Sir Ian) Botham made 81. Less grafting, but no less invaluable.

I had not yet found gainful employment (that job in a pizza place could wait) and so on the fifth day I drifted down to Lord's. England had the temerity to declare early on the fifth day, leaving the West Indies needing 342 to win. Forget it! An impossible run chase. The only likely winners were England. They had the best part of a day to bowl the West Indies out and there didn't seem to be any danger that their opponents could make the 342 required for victory. Prior to that match there had been nearly 1,000 Test matches. In only four of those had a team successfully chased down a fourth innings total of more than 342 to win. The highest was 406, which India managed in Port of Spain in 1976.[12] And besides, England had Ian Botham. This was to be his Test. In the first innings he had taken eight for 103.

[12] The West Indies have since surpassed this. They chased 418 to beat Australia in 2003

His best figures ever in a Test innings and the first time an England player had taken eight wickets in an innings against the West Indies. Then he had scored all those runs on a hostile pitch. The gods were smiling on him. As the *Guardian* put it, 'not even Richards had made batting look easy'.

Ah, yes, the great Viv Richards. I had heard about him. I was looking forward to seeing him bat. But not even he was expected to be able to delay England's inevitable victory. And even if England didn't win, if the West Indians stuck around long enough to force a draw, even then there was no chance of them chasing down a fourth innings deficit of 342. On a pitch that had yielded little more than 200 runs a day for the previous four days? Forget it. Never going to happen.

I arrived just after the start of play. It was a warm day and back then you could sit on the grass next to what is now the Compton Stand. I found a spot just behind the picket fence and settled in to watch. Gower had declared and the West Indies were just coming in to bat. There wasn't much of a crowd, but it was big enough for us to hear the hush of anticipation as Willis and Botham warmed up for the expected onslaught.

Except the onslaught came from the other side. In the most astonishing piece of batting I have ever witnessed (the other was Mike Atherton making 185 not out at the Wanderers in 1996, but that was a wholly different kind of batting), Gordon Greenidge proceeded to treat the England bowlingwith something that went way beyond contempt. He made 214 at just under one run per ball. The only wicket to fall was Desmond Haynes, who was run out by Allan Lamb when the South African scored a direct hit from square leg. Larry Gomes hung around for an excellent 92 not out, but the day and the match and my memory belong to Greenidge.

'Was he, like, famous?' asked the boy.

Well, not then. Not really. I mean, he was an international cricketer and that is saying something. Plenty of people knew him. In that sense he was famous. But he hadn't yet set the cricket world alight and I didn't know anything about him then. And that's the complicated part. For me the fact that I didn't know him was a good thing. The fact that I knew nothing about him – and the fact that he was playing at all – also meant that he was not one of the West Indian cricketers who took part in the rebel tour of South Africa a year and a half before. My knowledge of West Indian cricketers was confined entirely to those who had come to Cape Town in the summer of 1982–83. They were the only ones I had heard of, and the hearing was entirely negative. We had a song we sang, an amalgamation of the growing resistance to service in the apartheid army and the street politics of boycott:

Turn your bows and arrows
Into hoes and barrows.
Grow oats and marrows,
And share them with the poor
And boycott the West Indies cricket tour...

Oh dear. Was I singing that aloud? The boy is looking at me with a mixture of horror and amusement.

'What was that?' he says with a grin. My daughter's grin; I've seen her do it exactly the same way. Lopsided, querying and indulgent all at once. The kind of smile you have just before you ask 'Does he take sugar?' And before you get yelled at for asking.

'Sorry,' I mumble. This wasn't quite what I had in mind. I didn't see myself as the one who should apologise.

'No, I like it,' he says.

Which is nice of him. No one, not even my girlfriend, has said that about my singing before.

'Well, we used to sing it,' I say. 'I mean, not me...' (He smiles) '... but other people. Back then.'

Back then. Before he or my daughter were born. They belong to the post-apartheid generation. To the 50 per cent of the population born since Mandela emerged from prison to address the crowds on the Grand Parade in Cape Town.

In 1983 I still wasn't playing cricket, but it had begun to resurface in my consciousness. I can't quite place the trajectory. It wasn't as if I had a team I followed. I was living in Cape Town then and Western Province, with its entertaining attack led by Keppler Wessels, Peter Kirsten, Garth Le Roux and Stephen Jeffries, were on show at Newlands. But it didn't grip me. Nor did the English rebels who came earlier in the year. They were captained by Geoffrey Boycott, which made for an easy target. 'Boycott Boycott!' we said and I did. But for some reason the West Indians were more interesting. Maybe it was that their reputations preceded them. Maybe it was because they were black and therefore if they won it would be a bloodied nose for (white) South African cricket. Or maybe it was just that cricket's a funny game. It never lets you go.

Of course I boycotted the West Indian rebel tour as well. Equally (of course?) I couldn't resist. I was teaching in a place called Mitchell's Plain at the time, a so-called 'coloured' township near Cape Town. My journey to and from work took me past the beautiful cricket ground at Newlands and coming home in the afternoons I could never resist the tempting branch of an oak tree, accessible from the platform of Newlands Station, from which I would watch the cricket. I mean, it was okay, wasn't it? If I wasn't paying, I wasn't supporting it. Was I?

The boy had no view on the politics of boycott.

'Oh,' he says. 'I wasn't even born then.'

Which makes it a history so ancient it should be in books.

We enter by the north gate, even though our tickets are for seats on the far side of the ground. The turnstiles are a bit of a problem with the crutches, but the boy manages to squeeze through. He waits patiently while we're patted down by the security guards. They search the bag I have brought, clearly more interested in whether I am exceeding the alcohol quota than whether I am carrying a gun. The ground has changed since I first came. Back in 1984 it was dominated by the old Pavilion to the west and the Grand Stand to the north. The Pavilion – designed by Thomas Verity and now a listed building – was started in 1889 and completed in time for the following season. But neither the giant Mound Stand, with its hospitality suites and elegantly cantilevered roof, nor the more prosaic Edrich and Compton Stands, were in existence.

Now the playing field is completely surrounded. You can't see it as you walk in from the gates. All you see are the rather unlovely backsides of the various stands. I find I am ahead of the boy and I realise that he has stopped to look in wonder. Also to navigate the crowd with his crutches. A first-day crowd. Men taking the day off. Members sporting their MCC ties for the first time. Young Australians looking wide-eyed at the self-proclaimed home of cricket... It occurs to me for the first time that he really does want to be here. He is not doing it to please me. He is doing it for himself and despite my daughter. Despite *his* girlfriend.

'Come on,' I say to the boy. 'They'll be on soon.'

A warm sigh of satisfaction has gone round the crowd. Start of play was delayed by the rain, but now the covers are coming off. Another ten minutes and the players will be on the field. The boy and I continue to wind through the crowd behind the Grand Stand. I am the scythe; I cut a path through which he can follow. The thing about cricket, more than any sport, is it is a team game that allows for individual greatness. Other sports – rugby, football, hockey – there may be moments of brilliance. Or one person may play a blinder. May do something that changes the course of a match. Score a goal or make a tackle or pierce the defence with a pass so accurate and calculated and visionary that it changes everything. But in the end it is still team effort. In cricket, however, one man cannot only change everything, he can 'be' everything. An individual performance can be so dominant, so peerless, that the match, the entire spectacle, the entire narrative becomes the story of that one person. Think of Botham's Ashes. (Does Bob Willis resent this? He bowled them out...) Think of Lara's 400 not out. Or think of the Lord's Test of 1984.

One of the West Indian players in the 1982/83 rebel tour of South Africa was Alvin Greenidge. I remembered little of him. His Test career had been modest; his rebel tour more so. So when his namesake came down the stairs and took strike, I was not expecting fireworks. Nobody was. How could we have been prepared for what was about to happen? This was a fifth-day pitch in a low-scoring match. By the natural order of things the West Indies would be rolled up in short order and the series could move on to Headingley neatly poised at 1-1.

No such luck. The West Indies started slowly. They can't have scored more than ten off the first half-hour. And then Greenidge decided enough was enough. He laid into England's increasingly ragged attack with a brutality and confidence that made a mockery of his team's precarious position. Cricket's a strange game that way. England knew – we all knew – that a wicket could change everything. 'One brings two' is the mantra fielding sides repeat when batsmen go on the rampage. It only takes ten balls to dismiss an entire side. It takes five or six hundred to make 341. And yet somehow the dismissals never seemed likely. Even when Haynes was run out with the score on 60 odd, nobody looked like getting out. You could hear the England players chirping in the field (an advantage of a less than capacity crowd) but you didn't need to hear them to see what was happening. Shoulders sagged. Hands strayed to pockets. Botham dropped Greenidge (catches are also personal; he didn't drop the ball, he 'dropped Greenidge') shortly after the batsman had reached his century. It didn't seem to matter. If he got out then Viv Richards – Sir Viv, these days – would have come in. And Richards with the scent of victory in his patrician nostrils would make Greenidge look dull. Nobody could take an attack apart like him.

Suddenly there was no place for England to hide. The runs mounted. Botham, who had taken eight for 103 in the first innings, now bowled twenty overs, took no wickets and was hit for 117 runs. Nearly six an over! And most of them from Greenidge. Even the edged six with which he brought up the double hundred looked like he meant it. It was brutal stuff. It took a team on the verge of regaining some confidence and destroyed them for the rest of the series. Frank Keating put it neatly in the *Guardian*: 'As climaxes go it was one heck of an anti-climax for England. Before our very eyes Botham's match became Greenidge's. Of the nine Test double hundreds scored at Lord's none can have so cruelly suggested candy-from-kids. In his long peaked cherry cap pulled jauntily low over his hangdog moustache Greenidge looked like a sadistic uncle enjoying an afternoon's beach cricket against his nephews and nieces back home in Barbados...'

The transition is marked by the name given to the match. Not Botham's but Greenidge's. What made it more poignant still was that, of all the players in that great West Indian team, Greenidge had a perfect claim to being English. Much more than, say, Lamb. Or me. But he chose to play for the West Indies and never before or since has he done it with such command – and such effect.

'Can I ask you something?' says the boy. We had got as far as the back of the Pavilion. Walking through a crowd on crutches is not easy.

'Sure.'

'Why does it mean so much to you?'

'What, Lord's?'

'Well, I suppose. But that match? I mean, it was just a game of cricket?'

I suppose it was. But I was a young man in search of a team. A young man in search of heroes. In South Africa I had followed domestic cricket avidly enough. In South Africa it was possible to love the game but not the people. Rugby, curiously, was a more democratic game. At university I played Sunday league with a mixed-race team based at a bottle store on the front line between Cape Town's white and coloured suburbs. We were managed by the bottle-store owner. Half the team were his coloured workers and half were odd white or black students he had recruited from here and there. We played with passion and verve and generally got thumped. But it was fun and the deathly odour of apartheid could, briefly, be forgotten. But rugby was never my sport. It lacked the literature. It lacked the silences. There was no space for poetry. For grace and strength and power and courage, yes. But for poetry? And so with this confused sporting heritage I had come to London, to find myself, to find a home and – with any luck – to find a cricket team to support.

'But your team were getting thrashed?'

'Well, yes, but...'

But what? But they weren't quite mine. Not yet. And while it was true that they were getting thrashed, it was also true that they were doing it in style. It is not easy to lose as spectacularly as England lost that day. And it is not easy to smile – as Gower did – when the crowd ran on to the field with their 'blackwash' banners. And it's not easy to move on to the next match and do it all again. If England had won – as expected – that day, would I have liked them as much? I doubt it, even though I hadn't yet learned to laugh. Or not to laugh. Or – which is what supporting England really requires – to do both at the same time.

The boy is smiling to himself. For a moment I think he is sharing the pathos of my anecdote. Actually he is looking at a text message on his phone. It must be break at my daughter's school. Unless she was texting in class. In which case I could expect another dressing down at 4 pm the following day.

'How is she?' I ask.

But he is too busy texting her to reply to me.

I LOVE . . .

The dialectic of materialism

There's a guy I used to know, a big wheel in the television industry, who took me sailing. A wild west wind ripped across the Atlantic and tossed bathfuls of water into our waiting eyes. My stomach heaved and my nose ran. His yacht, a beautiful thing in racing green, sliced through the mountainous waters. And he stood grinning wildly. I hadn't seen someone quite so high since my brother raided a beehive and ate three or four kilos of raw honey at a sitting. He was like a helium balloon that had torn free of its mooring. Floating high and wild on a wind. Who knew where he would land?

I was standing next to him at the helm.

'As close to heaven as I get,' he yelled above the noise of lanyard on mast, of wind in sail. Of water up my nose. 'Worth every penny.'

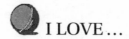

Earlier, on land, in safety, back when I was happy, we'd discussed the price of sailing. He'd trotted out the old line about it being like standing in a cold shower, tearing up £50 notes. And then he told me about the chandler's shop on Shaftesbury Avenue. Arthur Beale it's called and everybody knows it. It's one of those places that rise above change. It has been there since the dawn of time. Four or five hundred years, they say. Even though the water is a mile or two away. It's one of those shops that keeps people coming back. A proper chandlery with properly trained staff who know what they're talking about. An absolute must for all aficionados of all things maritime. And a proper place to waste – sorry – spend money.

It lay directly on my friend's route to work.

'One hundred and seventy-three pounds,' he said. 'Every time I go in that place it costs me one hundred and seventy-three pounds. Don't know what I buy. Don't know why. I just know that if I go in, I'm not going to get out for less than that.'

Not the big stuff – the yacht and the mast, the sails and the navigation stuff. Just the little things. Cleats and lazy jacks, cordage and shackles. Sail stops. Sailing stuff. And every time he goes in he waves his credit card and acquires more stuff. For £173, give or take a couple of hundred quid.

I reckon the Lord's shop sets me back about half that. Not disastrous – it's not on my route to work (unless you count writing this book, which my girlfriend definitely doesn't, in which case watching cricket is 'work') – but it all adds up. Which is why I try not to go too often. Because I have everything I need. A bat. Some pads. A box. Gloves, flannels, shirt, boots, bag. Keeper's gloves (we'll get to my keeping fantasy in a minute), keeper's pads. Inners. Keeper's inners. Balls, bails, stumps. Scorebook (just in case). Kookaburra polycarbonate Genesis pro-sportsman's sunglasses. (Never worn, on account of my other glasses, the ones I actually need to be able to see.) Spare studs. Spare spikes. Spike key. And the same again for my son. Plus the tat. Small balls, autograph bats, scorecards.

And the books. The endless, wonderful, delusional world of cricket books…

What I don't have is a helmet, even though I should really. My son does – but he only wears it when 'good people' are bowling to him. Which apparently doesn't include me. Or didn't. A couple of weeks back he got braces put in to straighten out a couple of wayward teeth. We went straight to the nets. I bowled, shortish, slowish on leg stump. He stepped back and across (nice one) and top edged it into his teeth. Not so nice. The teeth stayed intact (it was a slow ball) but a couple of brace pads fell off (it wasn't that slow).

'You should have worn your helmet,' I said.

'I should have hit you for six,' he replied.

Orthodontist's bills notwithstanding, cricket is a reasonably cheap sport. Not quite as cheap as football, but still cheap. Definitely at the low end of the investment scale. You don't need a boat or a horse or a stable or a bicycle that costs you two or three grand, and that's before you put brakes on the thing. You don't need a boat or petrol or a car. You don't need to fly to Aspen or St Moritz. It's surprisingly light on consumables, too. There's the ball, of course, which is a match expense. And there's the upkeep of the grounds, which can be shared. But beyond that? The stuff you used last week will be fine for next week. The kit that served you so well last season will be okay come next April. Even your bat, supposing you look after it properly, will last a good few years. Knock it in well, oil it properly (but not too much, and not on the splice) and store it in a dry, cool place – and you'll get years of good use out of it. The same goes for your pads. And your boots. My current pair are entering their sixth season. I reckon they've got another six in them. There's a guy I know who's been wearing the same boots for 25 years. Playing something like 25 games a season. The toes are gone, some studs are missing and the heels are shot to pieces, but he won't change them. Not for anything – and I'll tell you why. It's because in 1984, a week after he bought them, he scored a 50 in those boots. The only 50 he's ever scored. The only 50 he's likely ever to score. But he did it once and he did it in these boots a week after he bought them. They're his lucky boots and nothing you can say will change his mind. Not the smell. Not 25 years of subsequent failure. Not even the fact that, a couple of weeks ago, he was run out because he tripped over the flapping sole of his left boot.

There's no such danger for the players as they come down the Pavilion steps at Lord's for the start of the first Test of the 2007 season. Spectators emerge from the dark alleys behind the field into the perfect arena for international cricket. I cannot be the first to liken it to entering a church. The passage from dark into light makes the comparison irresistible. And for the players it is something even more special. A lateral arabesque from the Sistine Chapel of the Pavilion to the St Peter's of the field.

Our seats are in the Mound Stand and as we crest the stairs and look out onto the sparking field, the first sunlight of the day breaks through the grey, heavy clouds overhead. The covers are off and play will start in a few minutes. I have been to Lord's when there is a crowd (if that's the word) of 300. And I have been there when it is packed to the rafters. Current capacity is around 30,000 although there are plans to increase it. It doesn't seem to matter how many people are there. It always sounds the same. So much so that the press have long since given it a name: the Lord's murmur, a sound unlike any other at any other sporting occasion. It is the hum of what – of anticipation? Of friendship? Of history? Take Ben Dirs again: 'Almost full now at Lord's and the murmur is threatening to turn into a buzz. And when there's a buzz at Lord's, the security folk start getting a bit twitchy. A "buzz" at Lord's is the equivalent to a full-scale riot at an American music festival.'

It may threaten, but does it ever make good the threat? Perhaps at Twenty20 games when they play rock music every time someone hits a boundary. Perhaps had the last Test been played there instead of at the Oval when England won the Ashes in 2005. Maybe then the murmur would have become something more, a raucous demonstration of delight. The kind of sound you associate with the Wanderers or Sabina Park or the Wankhede Stadium in Mumbai or – indeed – with Lord's in 1984 before they priced or legislated the famously raucous and celebratory West Indian fans out of the game. But generally? Generally not. Generally the Lord's murmur rises and falls like an inland sea. It has Matthew Arnold's 'tremulous cadence slow' of the pebbles on Dover Beach but not their 'melancholy, long, withdrawing roar'. It is the lapping of waves and like the pebbles it will 'begin, and cease and then again begin'. But unlike Arnold we find in the thought not the desperate decline of faith, but its renewal. It is the sound of the Mediterranean not the Atlantic. It is the whisper of a summer breeze amongst ancient oaks. It is the tinkle of glasses and the loosening of ties. It is the shuffling of newspapers. It is the sound of people thinking.

And it is the sound of rumours. They come thick and fast from the seats all around us. Monty has been chosen in preference to Jimmy Anderson. Or has not been chosen. There is talk about the weather. The covers are off. Play will start in ten minutes. Or fifteen minutes. Or an hour. There is more rain forecast. It's going to clear. There is rain at Heathrow. The queen is coming. The queen is not coming. Did you hear old Tom is getting a divorce from his wife. No, not that one, the other one. She's something in the city, so he should be alright. Maybe she'll be the one paying alimony. Ho, ho, ho. The Lord's murmur. A bit like the sound of assent in its namesake across town. I sat in the Strangers Gallery once and listened not to the debate but to the shuffling of papers and the gentle murmur of Members whispering to each other while the business of the house continued at its deathly slow pace.

The boy and I smile and apologise our way to our seats. It's hard work with the crutches and there are some casualties. An early morning pint here, a copy of the *Telegraph* there.

'Sorry,' we say.

'Not at all,' come the replies. Even from the bloke whose spilled pint is now dripping onto the stashed leather briefcase of the man in the dark suit. Who is clearly bunking off work but will have to run to a meeting later.

'So what now?' he asks.

Now the umpires appear followed closely by the West Indians. Then Strauss and Cook. At least they're easy to tell apart. Strauss is stocky and tense. Cook is fluid and patrician.

'So now we watch.'

In silence. It's slow, but not unpleasant.

Italy, 1998

We are on holiday which means that we have more time than usual to write my daughter's diary. She's recently started to take an interest in it. She proofreads it for accuracy and veracity. She criticises my choice of adjectives. She berates me for not giving my girlfriend a more prominent role.

'Well, you write it then,' I say.

Some chance. At lunch we sit in the Italian sun and eat salami, tomatoes, grapes and pistachio nuts. My daughter is smiling to herself. She turns to her brother and sister and says, *sotto voce*, 'I wonder which one of them will be the first to say, "This is the life"?'

It's not just that we are watching her grow up. It is that she is watching us, and doing it more closely, more acutely – more intelligently? – than we ever will. 'Certainly you intended to tease us,' I wrote that night, 'and certainly you intended the remark half as a question because once we had recovered from our laughter you went on to ask why we always say that.'

The conversation moved on. There was a time when my father was in the leather business. His travels took him occasionally to Italy where 'they make the best shoes in the world'.

'Oh, good,' says my daughter. 'Can I have some?'

We visited seven shoe shops that afternoon. By the time we had finished I had purchased a stout pair of handmade leather walking shoes. And she had, well, nothing. We had not been able to agree on anything worth buying...

'Tomorrow I'm going with Mum,' she said. 'She knows how to shop.'

As against which I would say only that even now I have my stout pair of Italian walking shoes. Whereas the bright and shiny sandals she bought? Where are they now?

At lunch Cook and Strauss have passed their 50 partnership in comfort. The West Indian attack looks ordinary – I say that in the full knowledge that if Collymore, Edwards or any of the rest ever bowled to me I would be lucky to see, let alone hit, a ball – and the crowd were nodding off gently.

Other commentators – ones who have faced better bowling – were less kind. 'Hapless' was one description. 'Absolutely dire' another. 'Like drips,' said Geoffrey Boycott. It doesn't matter much. At lunch England look in control at 85 without loss. Cook is playing fluently and Strauss – well, he isn't fluent, but he is playing. It doesn't matter much to the boy. He's not really following the cricket. He's looking around at the architecture. Sizing up the different stands. From time to time he asks me when one was built. The Pavilion? 1890. The Mound Stand? 1987. The Media Centre? Stirling Prize, 1999. But I'm not sure that the dates in which stands were built is really the essence of cricket. There must be something else.

'Come on,' I say. 'Let's go see what they've got in the shop.'

Like I didn't know. Like I had forgotten my daughter's final words as she left for school that morning.

'And don't buy him stuff,' she had said.

'Why not?' I asked.

Her look told me all I needed to know:

a) My taste was crap and
b) Buying him 'stuff' was her prerogative. She had recently sewn up the babysitting rackets in our neck of the woods. Several families depended on her services. She was therefore feeling the early inklings of power that came with a healthy bank balance. She didn't want me messing with this delicate ecosystem by waving my credit card at the brightly packaged goods available in the Lord's shop.

'I don't want him to feel he owes you.'

'He already owes me,' I said. I meant for the filming. I

meant for the hours spent in casualty. I meant for the mountain of food provided over the weeks. I meant for her.

'You broke his foot,' she said, which apparently cancelled all debts. Even though it wasn't true.

Lunchtime at the Lord's shop is mostly about window shopping. Only without the window between you and the goods. Men in pinstripe suits take bats off the rack and (insofar as the cramped lunchtime rush-hour conditions allow) practise shots they have never played. I blame Strauss actually. Strauss has an endearing habit of wandering out to the middle before his innings starts and visualising the balls he is going to have to face. He takes guard carefully. He takes his stance, just the way he does in a match. Slightly open, shoulder pointing at mid-on, feet apart, eyes ahead. He watches the imaginary bowler run up and he plays an imaginary ball. He turns this one down leg for a single. He strokes that one to mid-off. He plays back to the next one. He lets this one go through to the keeper. It's the cricket equivalent of air guitar. He's hearing a music all of his own. Belting out stadium rock to an audience of one. To watch him – I've seen it speeded up on DVD as well – is to imagine his whole innings. Only difference is, in the practice version he never goes only half forward to a fullish delivery outside off stump. And he never gets caught at slip.

It's not only the men. Women in twin sets and pearls hunt for possible birthday gifts. Lord's helpfully has its memorabilia classified by price. Under a tenner. £10 to £25. £25 to £50. Over £50. Well, what's it going to be? *How deep*, as the Bee Gees said all those years ago, *is your love*? Is your man worth the price of a £20 bottle of Lord's scotch? Or will he give you a lot of grief about single malt this and peaty that? At least it's cheaper than the Thomas Lord teddy bear. Yours for a pony, as they say on TV.

And behind the wives there are the boys in replica shirts fingering the latest version, the one their fathers won't buy them on account of

a) they cost £40 and
b) they've got one from last season, even if it is a hand-me-down from their brother.

And then there are visitors from Australia or South Africa balking at the prices and muttering darkly about exchange rates and rip-offs. And suckers like me pulling out our credit cards.

Despite our daughter's advice.

I mean, I had to buy him something. To remember the day by. A memento. The question was what? Actual kit would probably be going too far. I mean, what would he do with a pair of keeping pads? Ideally, of course, he would give them to me. I share a pair with my son – and they are too big for him and too small for me. I could use some more. But no, this wasn't about me. It was about... well, okay, maybe it was about me. Just a little bit.

To buy him a bat – the usual starting point for cricket – was a bit extreme. Tricky purchases, actually, bats. Hard to tell what you're getting. In theory a cricket bat is like wine: you get what you pay for. Pay a fiver for some plonk and you get plonk. Fork out 50 quid a bottle and you get – well, wine that's worth more than £5 a bottle. And may just be worth the full £50. So probably not a bat.

Replica gear? I don't think so. I have never liked the stuff. Rip-off deluxe, out of date with each passing season and – besides – it makes you look like all those Barmy Army lunatics, the ones who are gently amusing in the morning and a pain in the neck when they're pissed and depressed at five in the evening. (Sorry, dear Barmy Army. I'm sure you're lovely. It's just that I'm, well, getting old. And you do make a racket. And it's often dull. And your wit is many things, but witty ain't one of them.) Books. I steer him towards the books. Subtly, so he won't notice.

Too subtle by half. He glides past the bookshelves and arrives at the bats. He takes down a particularly expensive Gray-Nicolls, a beautiful bat, the kind of thing I might buy if I were rich. Or any good. He runs his hand over it, the way he might run his hand over... well, never mind what else he has been running his hand over. He holds it up to his nose and smells the clean willow. He sights along the slight bow of the blade. He feels the weight. He takes a stance, but (slight grin, faint blush) doesn't try a shot. I am in a generous mood. I don't tell him his stance is a lot like John Major's.

'Nice,' he says.

Expensive, I think.

'How do they make them?' he asks.

I had no idea.

'Only,' he says. 'I've been making a board.'

Just like that, from nowhere. A fully formed thought in a fully formed sentence. With a subject, verb, object and everything. Followed by a flood of them.

'The hard part is getting the balance right. I want it to be stiff, but not too stiff.'

Oh.

'It depends what wood you use. You get different laminates. At school they let us use the workshops. Steam-pressed ash seems to work best. But it's quite hard to get right. We had to make a mould.'

Was my mouth open? I suspect so. Did a sound come out? Not a chance.

We – I – settle for a ball. Not a bad idea. Always nice to have, a cricket ball. Something very satisfying about a ball. It fits your hand so well. It is hard and shiny and has a smell that appeals no doubt to the same part of a man's brain that thinks Lynx is an attractive smell. I steer him gently in the direction of the balls. And (slightly less gently) point him towards the ones that cost £8.99, but which look exactly the same as the ones that cost £25. But, hey, he's never going to play with it and, besides, it's got the Lord's logo on it. What more does he want?

'Thanks,' he says.

'You're welcome. You should get it autographed.'

'Why?'

Well, actually I'm not sure. Why do boys chase autographs?

'It's the thing to do,' I say.

'Oh.'

Normal service has been resumed.

I LOVE …

Watching the watchers

But a seed has been sown. The germ of an idea. A little thing, taking root in the fertile soils of my mind. It just needs a little sunshine to make it grow. Unfortunately we don't have sunshine. What we have is an early frost.

'You bought him a what?' I'm grinning too much to answer, so my daughter turns her attention to her boy.

'He bought you a what?' Her voice is a shard of ice in an echoing cave.

'It's got an autograph,' he says. Like that's going to get him off the hook.

'Who?'

Which had him stumped.

'Collymore,' I say. Who kindly signed the ball during a lull in proceedings.

'Yeah,' he says. 'Him.'

'For heaven's sake,' says my daughter.

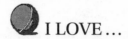

It is the essence of watching Test cricket that we each experience our own match. My Test match is not Michael Vaughan's Test match. Nor is it the match described by the commentators up in their gallery. Nor is it the match of the thousands of words that pour forth from the rather startling and extremely beautiful Media Centre at the Nursery End at Lord's. And nor is it the match of the boy next to me who was watching for the first time. I would like it to be, but it isn't. We each have our own. We experience it differently and remember it differently. My memory of the first day of the first Test at Lord's is not about cricket at all. Nor is it about this young man in whose company I find myself. It is not the motorcycle ride or the ticket price or the indifferent, blustery threatening weather. For me that first day of the first Test was about my daughter.

'Why does he text so much?' I had asked in jest earlier in the week.

'Because he loves me,' she replied also in jest.

'How's the prisoner?' she texted during a school break. 'Are you feeding him?'

Well, no, we only just arrived.

'He is alive,' I say. An old joke from an old friend. His perennial answer to the question of 'How are you?' But serious also. He is of an age when to be alive is statistically unlikely. I send my daughter a picture of the boy with the front page of today's *Guardian*. Just like real kidnappers do to show their prisoner is alive.

It costs a lot of money to spend a day at Lord's. In the 2008 season, tickets for Test matches started at £60. And if you're foolish enough to buy your food or your drinks from the concession stands in the ground you can easily spend double that in a day. Perhaps for the same reason, Lord's is one of the few grounds where you are allowed to bring your own food and drink into the ground. 'They treat you like grown-ups,' Jonathan Agnew said on *Test Match Special*. 'And funnily enough they don't have any crowd trouble.'

It was an indifferent sort of day. Darkly massing clouds above. The threat of rain in the air. We had got spattered by a little rain on the way there and arrived to find the covers just coming off. It was looking like being a stop-start day. One of those ones where you wish you had brought a good book. Or a crossword. Or a companion who speaks.

'So how did you two meet?' I ask, even though I sort of know. Like a good journalist, I wanted a second opinion.

The boy is not forthcoming.

'Oh, God,' he says, with the weariness of those who have seen the world and found it wanting. 'It was a long time ago.'

London 1994

I have a friend who used to get his children to sleep by standing at Clapton roundabout in east London. The mesmerising effect of headlights swooping past through a gloomy London night never failed them. 'I used to walk them through the cemetery,' he said, 'but after a while it gave me the creeps.'

We have never had this difficulty. From the start our daughter has loved her sleep and she will nod off anywhere. In the car, on her bed, strapped into her bicycle seat. She has a helmet and it acts as a pillow. Her hands flap over the armrests, like she's giving contradictory signals to the passing traffic. But my most common diary entry is also my favourite: 'Tonight you fell asleep in my arms,' I wrote two or three times a month. 'It's one of the great pleasures.' There is a moment when a person goes to sleep when their breath slows, and when they give themselves over completely to whatever the gods or the fates may hold for them. And yet some instincts for survival remain. Before she nods off my daughter grips my finger tightly and in the early stages of her sleep her grip does not lessen. And then, for five or ten or twenty minutes, for however long I have before the demands of the real world encroach, I sit and watch her sleep.

I have to prise her finger away to put her down on the bed.

London 2007

'So that's it?' says the boy as we take our seats after lunch. He is studying his new cricket ball minutely. Trying to decipher the scrawl masquerading as an autograph. Picking at the seam like an old pro trying to get a bit more turn on a slow day at Uxbridge.

Well, no, not quite. That's not quite it. Just the opening salvo. Just the first shots. A bit slow, I admit, but that's Test cricket for you. It's not a game of wham, bam, thank you ma'am. You've got to let it build. Let the narrative swell. It could still go either way. Today it has been England's morning, certainly, but a couple of quick wickets after lunch will swing it the West Indies way.

'Just starting,' I say. 'Just getting warmed up.'

And sure enough, there is a moment's excitement after lunch. Strauss out. Caught off Powell for 33. Waving his bat outside off stump. A silly shot for a silly dismissal. But who am I to criticise? Shah comes in. He is a local hero, part of the Middlesex team. Capable of some truly spectacular hitting. In the one-day series against India later in the season he will hit a flat-bat six that goes as fast as any cricket ball I have ever seen. Today the crowd tries to get excited, but Shah is not looking in great touch. He scratches around a bit, manages to nick one and is out for six. Which, secretly, is what the crowd wants. Because it means that Pietersen is coming to the crease. Another South African. From my home town of Pietermaritzburg. Unlike the rest of his team-mates, Pietersen didn't have a bad series in Australia. He made 490 runs in five matches (second only to the Australian captain, Ricky Ponting) at an average of 54. Not bad in a series where your team is getting hammered. This is his first home Test since that tour. The big stage, the home of cricket, and no one likes a big stage more than Pietersen. The crowd senses it. I sense it – even the boy senses it.

'That's him?'

It is.

'Is he actually going to hit the ball?' In contrast, you understand, with Cook and Strauss, who have been nudging and nurdling for all they're worth. But Pietersen doesn't do nurdles. He starts by missing a straight one – almost an obligatory shot for him. And then he starts to hit. He 'whips' Collymore for four through mid-wicket. He strolls down the pitch to Powell and 'thumps' him (always personal; always so *very* personal) through extra cover. The commentator would have been struggling for verbs. You can read them on the websites where these things enjoy a strange and little-visited afterlife. But Pietersen was not struggling for shots. He first 'punches' and then 'flays'. Bravo.

The boy is enjoying it. There is something visceral about the crack of the ball on wood. There is something comic about the predictable crowd response. The oohs that turn into aahs. The gasp at Pietersen's arrogance.

'You having fun?' I ask.

'She should be here,' he says.

He texts her furiously. God only knows what he says. I try

to peek, but his hair hides the screen. For minutes on end there is no response. I should hope not. She's in lessons and should not be texting anyone. At which point my phone beeps. It's a text from my daughter.

'*Could you please talk to him?*' she writes. '*I do hope you're having fun, but please tell him to stop texting otherwise they will confiscate my phone. Explain that I am in biology and our teacher is particularly strict and while my love for him is great, I cannot see that it is in either of our interests that I should have my telephone confiscated. Or yours, for that matter, because you are the one who will have to go and get it and be reprimanded into the bargain on your inadequate parenting. I look forward to catching up when we get home.*' Only she doesn't put it quite like that. What she says is: 'Hvg fn? Cnt txt. Bio. L8er.'

'She's busy,' I say to the boy.

'Yeah.'

Our conversations wind down like the ball in a roulette wheel. It doesn't much matter where it lands. Nobody seems to win.

Which may be why the man next to me is asleep and snoring *basso profundo*. With each breath a little balloon of spittle forms in the corner of his flaccid mouth. His breathing is shallow and the bubble never quite has the energy to burst. It expands and subsides in comic imitation of his ample gut. With each intake of air the last drop of spit scuttles back into his mouth, like a length of sucked spaghetti. I expect it to flap round and leave a smear of tomato sauce on his upper lip. The boy wonder is watching it with reverent fascination. Much more fascination than he accorded the cricket. As the man snores the bubble forms again. Perhaps he had something fatty for lunch. The surface of the bubble is glazed with pastel mauves and blues, like an oil slick on a wet road. The boy reaches out with his forefinger. He pretends to pop the bubble, but catches my eye. I shake my head and he smiles. He was never going to. It was just a thought. The sleeping man seems to have sensed it though. He wakes with a start and looks around in confusion. In front of us the ground is empty. The players have come off for bad light beneath a glowering grey sky. We are seated in the lowest tier of the Mound Stand, which is at the southern edge of Lord's. His head wobbles precariously as he loses consciousness and then slips onto his chest. His straw hat slips forward on his head. He has a florid complexion and is running a little to fat. The gossamer web of red lines are mute testimony to his toper's past. Perhaps he is dreaming. He gives a little grunt of satisfaction followed by a strange little yip. He reminds me of an old dog we had, sleeping by the fire. It occurs to me suddenly that here, now, he is completely happy. Whatever it is he does in the world, and whoever he does it with, has slipped away. His only concern is the cricket and in the absence of cricket he has no concerns at all. He appears to be alone. He is wearing a pale cream suit with a faint purple pinstripe. The stripe matches his socks, but not his blue shirt or the burgundy handkerchief peeping untidily from his pocket. He has on worn brown Oxford shoes and a tie stained with the detritus of one meal too many. On his lap a copy of *The Times* is folded open at the crossword, which is roughly half done. His snore has become loud to the point of being embarrassing. Behind us an Australian woman who has spent the afternoon gamely trying to make it a fun day for her corporate clients makes a lewd joke. The men – her clients – laugh loudly, but the man beside us does not stir. For that we need something more subtle. It happens shortly afterwards.

The 'Lord's murmur' is the sum of a thousand slow conversations. What happens now to stir our sleeper is a slight shift in the pitch and tone of the murmur. It moves from 'nothing happening' to 'something happening'.

'Something happening' turns out to be a few blue blazers massing at the door to the Pavilion. From our seats in the Mound Stand we can just make out the shapes moving behind the dark glass. Around us people begin to stand up. The man next to us wakes up with a start. Again he looks around.

'Something happening,' I say.

'About time,' he grunts. He wipes away his spit on the sleeve of his jacket and tries to stand up. As he does so, his copy of *The Times* slips to the ground to reveal a concealed copy of the *Sun*.

Something has happened. We all watch the England team stride down the steps. They are wearing blazers over their cricket clothes. They take the field and then mill about, uncertain what to do. Moments later the West Indies team appears. They are less cohesive and appear in dribs and drabs, but soon all twelve players are on the field. They are followed by a smattering of officials. One man in a blazer gives instructions. They form two lines, one of either side of the steps. The officials gather at the end of this guard of honour. Taken together there are perhaps 40 people there. The shape they have formed looks like an ice-cream cone.

'Must be royalty,' says my neighbour. 'Why else the blazers?'

We speculate as to what sort of royalty. A prince. The queen herself? Nobody seems to know. There have been no official announcements. The public address system is quiet. The announcements on the scoreboards remind us only that it is a crime of the worst sort to enter the playing area. The players do not seem to know what to do either. They stand uncomfortably. Pietersen and Cook, who were in when bad light stopped play, still have their pads on and look slightly ridiculous. Hoggard is having a bad hair day, but it is not clear that he has any other sort. Bell appears to have sunk into some kind of trance-like state and Strauss, the captain in the absence of the injured Vaughan, is glancing expectantly – nervously? – up the stairs to the Pavilion. Suddenly an official peels away from the waiting line and runs towards the centre of the ground. He stops at the pile of sawdust placed there to repair damage done to a damp pitch by the bowlers' pounding feet and scoops up two handfuls. Being careful to drop as little as possible, he trots back to the bottom of the stairs and places the sawdust there.

The crowd cheers ironically. It was good to have something to watch. The cheers subside and the murmur returns to its normal placid level. People begin to sit again. The moment of excitement has come and gone. The man next to us picks up his newspapers. He takes his pen out as though intending to do the crossword, but his attention is momentarily drawn to the undoubted charms of the woman on page three. But then someone in the Pavilion starts clapping. Quickly it spreads again. A few people rise to their feet. The rest of us have little choice but to do the same if we want to see 'the action'.

'It is her,' says someone – and indeed it is. The Queen, clad in a splendid purple coat, walks slowly down the stairs. To my delight she carefully avoids the patch of sawdust placed Walter Raleigh-like at the bottom of the stairs. First the West Indian captain Sarwan and then Strauss introduce her to their players. In fact, though, she knows many of the England team already, for they all received honours after the successful Ashes series of 2005. What did she say to them? What did she say to Paul Collingwood? Collingwood played in the last match of the series, during which he made a total of seventeen runs. The decision to award MBEs to the entire team raised a few eyebrows at the time, but was wholly in keeping with the Blair government's ability to read the popular mood and respond with suitable sentimentality. Geoffrey Boycott was not amused and suggested that henceforth he would let his cat wear his MBE on the grounds that if Collingwood had earned one, it was no longer 'worth a damn'. I have some sympathy with this assessment notwithstanding the fact that Collingwood has scored several centuries since then. He even scored one the next day at Lord's. At the time of writing, however, he remains roughly 6,500 runs short of the 8,000 Boycott made in his career and which he deems to be roughly the benchmark before anyone should be considered for an honour that was worth a damn.

'Well, well,' says the man next to me. 'Herself. Worth the price of the ticket any day.'

Perhaps. The cricket, it must be said, has hardly justified the £108 it cost us – me – to get in. That's £9 per hour or one pence per ball, which compares very unfavourably with, say, a movie but is not bad when you put it against the price of a decent seat at Covent Garden. But we have examined the mathematics of this elsewhere. In a full day's cricket the ball is in play for only 27 minutes. At £2 per minute it's starting to look a little pricy.

The queen finishes shaking hands with the two teams and departs. The teams leave the field with her. The crowd claps and then – although this was only a few and not the whole crowd – boos. They do not think seeing the queen is worth the price of admission.

My future son-in-law is one of those booing.

'Why?' I ask. Out of curiosity, you understand, and not (necessarily) because I disapprove.

'My dad'll ask,' he says. 'He's a republican.'

I LOVE …

Linseed and willow

It's nearly a week later and he's back again. Speaking in fully formed sentences.

'I don't understand how the bat works,' he says. 'I mean, it's just a piece of wood, right?'

Well, yes. A piece of English willow, actually.

'But it has that springy feeling?'

He is standing in the hallway bouncing a ball on my bat – a ball, not his ball. His ball is at his house. On the mantelpiece, like a trophy. My daughter told me. He sights down the blade again. Notes how it has a slight bow. Runs his hand down the back of it. Inspects the splice. Notes the rubber running through the handle.

'It's to do with the compression of the wood,' I say. 'You compress the grain at the front so that it's hard, but the wood at the back is soft and that's what gives it "spring".'

'It's different with skateboards,' he says.

Yes, well, I'm sure it is. Just like My Chemical Romance is different from, say, Mozart.

'Tell you what,' I say, 'we could make one.'

Which was jumping in at the deep end, actually. I had always had this mild fantasy that I could make a cricket bat.

But that – like scoring a century – is not the same as actually doing it.

'Cool,' he says.

'Da-ad,' says my daughter.

'It'll be good,' I say. 'I mean, it's not like he can go anywhere. Not with his leg.'

Which (in case you had forgotten) was my fault.

The bed was made from pine; cricket bats are made from willow. There are laws about this sort of thing. You can't – tempted though I was – go off to Hampstead Heath and cut down the nearest willow. For a start, cricket bats are not made from the sort of willow you find next to the boating pond. For bats you need Salix alba caerulea – white willow. And secondly you can't just chop one down; you have to replace whatever you take. And a bat willow takes twenty years to grow, so it's a bit of a project. Plant now for 2029. Not much of a proposition, really. So if you want to make your own bat, what you do is get in touch with a farm in Essex. They've been going for more than 100 years and supply willow to most of the world's leading brands. And to middle-aged but determined men who sweet-talk them in the white heat of enthusiasm after a trip to Lord's.

'It's for my daughter's boyfriend,' I said to the lady who answered the phone.

'Oh,' she said. 'Most people say it's for their son.'

I let it pass.

She tells me that cricket bat willow was used for medicinal purposes long before it was used for cricket bats. At Lord's one of the gifts (at the more expensive end of the range) is a display of the 'history of the cricket bat'. The originals looked more like a hockey stick than a cricket bat. Later I find a book that tells me that the bark of the white willow is 'anti-inflammatory, antiseptic, astringent, diuretic, hypnotic, sedative and tonic'. Which is not bad for one tree. But mostly it has been known for years as a source of salicylic acid, the precursor to aspirin.

'Oh,' I say. 'We just want to make a bat.'

'You can do that too,' she says. I order the 'starter pack'. It consists of a lump – they call it a 'cleft' – of willow, together with a partially turned handle, a length of string (for the handle), a grip and a pot of glue. The 'cleft' is roughly twice the size of the bat it will (I hope) one day become.

The boy turns it over in his hand.

'We're going to need some help,' he says.

But first we go to Lord's. Over my daughter's protest.

'The Test was fun,' he says. (More protests.)

'This will be different,' I promise. 'You can come too?'

Fat chance. It's just the boy and me and my motorbike.

The Lord's of a county match is not the same place as the Lord's of a Test match. It's emptier, for a start. We wander through the near-silent stands. The murmur is still there, but this time it's a real murmur. Not the Test match hum. No excited speculation about team sheets or the state of the pitch. It's day two of a county game between Middlesex and Essex. Essex won the toss and chose to bat – always wise – and were duly rewarded by being 342 for seven at close of play the night before. The only Middlesex bowler to have any sort of luck was the Sri Lankan left-arm fast bowler, Chaminda Vaas (or, to use his full name, Warnakulasuriya Patabendige Ushantha Joseph Chaminda Vaas). In the quiet of a county game we're free to wander about the ground and admire Lord's slightly overblown sense of its history. All around it has posters and banners with people saying nice things about it. Like an author's dust cover. I like to imagine that the comments are edited, the way authors do. The review's assessment of 'a book so bad it's in a class of its own' becomes 'in a class of its own' when it appears on the jacket. 'There's nowhere on earth like it to play cricket,' says Andrew Flintoff. I like to think they elided the 'Thank God…' before 'There's…' 'As a boy I dreamed of playing at Lord's,' says Monty Panesar. 'But then I grew up'? But that's just me being stupid. The players know what they're talking about. 'It's the best place on earth to play cricket,' says Shane Warne and I believe him.

Then there's the honours board – which records all batsmen who have scored Test centuries and all bowlers who have taken 'five-for' in a Test. 'Seeing all the legends up on that board, you want to be part of it. It's a great honour, something you'll always remember,' says Paul Collingwood, whose name is up there twice. 'The honours boards in each dressing room are covered with the names of the game's greats,' says Angus Fraser. Himself included. Always a favourite of mine, Angus Fraser. Not fast, not scary. Not even threatening. But he couldn't half bowl on a line and length. And the wickets came as a result.

It's especially special (if that's the phrase) for English batsmen. 'For an England cricketer, it doesn't get any better than a hundred at Lord's,' said Matt Prior after he made a century on his Test debut. There are some players who seem to have a particular affinity for the ground. Graham Gooch holds the record with six Test centuries. Michael Vaughan has five and Allan Lamb four. Dilip Vengsarkar's record of three centuries is the best by a visitor. It's harder work for bowlers. They take five-fors less often than batsmen score centuries – but some do both. Only one of Ian Botham's fourteen Test centuries was scored at Lord's but he took five wickets in an innings there no fewer than eight times. Although of late it has become a bowler's nightmare. In the 2008 season, for example, there were no fewer than eight Test centuries scored on the placid Lord's pitch. For England, Vaughan, Pietersen and Bell. For New Zealand, Oram and for South Africa, Prince, Smith, McKenzie and Amla. By contrast only Vettori for New Zealand took a five-for in Lord's Tests in 2008. In 2007 there were six and in 2006 there were eight. The last six matches have ended in a draw because of the inability of bowlers to dismiss teams twice.

The 2008 South African Test at Lord's was particularly trying for bowling. South Africa followed on 346 runs behind. When a draw was declared two days later, they had reached 393 for three and each of their top three batsmen made a century. I recently went to a fund-raising dinner in the Long Room at Lord's. A beautiful Victorian masterpiece with a glorious view of the ground. During a break in proceedings my host beckoned me and a friend.

'Come on,' he said. 'I'll show you something.'

We took the stairs to the visitors' changing room. We all know it from the television shots. During tense moments of a Test match the cameras will cut away to the balcony. It's quite small. There's space for only a few people to sit there. The same applies to the room. I look up at the honours board. Gordon Greenidge is up there. So are the two other double centurions I've seen at Lord's. Graeme Smith in 2003 and Mohammad Yousuf in 2006. But what catches my eye is the results of the 2008 Test against South Africa. Four of them made hundreds.

'It's a tradition,' says my host. 'Obviously they can't get the names engraved immediately. That takes time. So what they do, before the batsman gets back after his innings, is they write the details on a piece of masking tape and put it up. The guy's name will be on the board before he makes it back to the changing room.'

And sure enough there are four names there, written by hand on four strips of masking tape. Each of them would have walked in from the field and seen their names up there on the board. Up there with the best of them. With Greenidge and Richards and Sobers. With Walcott, Headley and Bradman. Greenidge is the only name to appear on the boards in the England *and* the visitors' changing rooms. He played for MCC against the Rest of the World in 1987 and made 122 and this was counted as a 'home' game for the honours board.

Sentimental old sods, the Lord's people. Just like me.

Our path takes us along the northern edge of the ground past what the ground map demurely calls a 'betting facility' and the printing shop and into the dark shadows beneath the Grand Stand. The throng is thick at this point and we have not yet seen the ground. We're not in any hurry. There has been some rain – the same rain that flecked us as we drove along on the motorbike – and the covers are still on. We pause at the underside of the Compton Stand. There's one of the banners Lord's have hung up to remember great feats at Lord's. This one is about Graham Gooch. It gives the facts simply: Graham Gooch, 333 not out v. India. 27 July 1990.

'Who was Gooch?' asks the boy.

We think we know our game. I can't recall how many inane conversations I have had about cricket, how many ridiculous or wonderful pieces I have read in the papers. How many books. How many hours on the radio. Hours and hours and hours. I have not, oddly enough, watched that much cricket on television. Perhaps I should. It is a sport perfect for television. It fills up the time. It has a long history. Every match is its own mini-narrative. And the cameras, especially in these days of Hawk-Eye and wagon wheels, computer generated field settings and so on, can bring you closer to the game than you'll ever manage from the back of the Mound Stand at Lord's. But as you know, I prefer the radio. I prefer to imagine it. It makes the match more personal, somehow. It makes it mine. It reminds me of my childhood. They say that journalism has a thousand golden ages, each one encompassing the three or four years after the person writing about it first became a cub reporter in the *Byfleet Gazette*. It is the same with cricket. Cricket's golden age, for me, was 1973. After I learned to keep my elbow up and before television. After South Africa's international isolation. And when the generation of cricketers, the ones who beat Australia in 1970, were put out to international pasture. Barry Richards is around these days, doing his commentaries on radio and television and writing about cricket. My earliest cricket memory is the 140 he made at Kingsmead against Australia. In that match Graeme Pollock went on to make two hundred and something, but Richards was from my part of the world and so it was his century that stuck. Those were the only Test matches he played. Four matches, two hundreds, 508 runs and an average of 72.57. Curiously I have little memory of watching him play – I did, but it didn't stick in the mind. The ones I remember are the unlikely athletes. Mike Procter with his wrong-foot delivery. Eddie Barlow looking like the fat kid in glasses, the one who never got picked at school. And Vince van der Bijl, who would run in to bowl looking like a giraffe, his backside out at an odd angle, his long back held like the giraffe's neck.

My cricket reading is piecemeal, eclectic and – like my drive – lacking in a methodology likely to produce any predictable results. I prefer journalism to books and I browse in the collected ramblings of yesteryear. I tend to avoid biographies. They don't do much for me and it is hard not to be seduced by Gideon Haigh's slightly jaundiced view in *Silent Revolutions*: 'By an inexact count of my own bookshelves, 127 cricketers, coachers, umpires and administrators of the last two decades have written, initiated and/or endorsed 174 works of autobiography or approved biography in that time.' That was in 2006 and the trend continues. And, in Haigh's view at any rate, the logic is unsavoury: 'The main purpose of an autobiography today, however, is not so much to tell a story, set a record straight or bid a dignified adieu, but to create an image or a market presence that stakes out one's commercial territory.'

Every sports star knows that you don't have to be famous for long for someone to pop up from the woodwork to claim they sat next to you at school or snogged you behind the bike sheds or (if you are both famous and rich) gave your love child up for adoption when their offer of marriage was inexplicably refused. But I do read the papers. Endlessly and voraciously. The match report, the colour piece, the playe profile. The old coach's view on where the new coach is going wrong. The player's guest column, ghosted by some underling in the night. I read them all. No matter how nonsensical; no matter how much it sounds like something Polly Filler put together in an idle moment.

And so I know an awful lot – except I know nothing. Cricket is not facts and figures. For all its love affair with averages and 'stats', they are not cricket. Cricket is a feeling, an emotion. Cricket is a state of being. Cricket is... well, *personal.* I find I am slightly flummoxed by the boy's question. 'Who was Gooch?' Partly because of the past tense. Graham Gooch is still very much with us. I hear him often on the BBC. But mostly because I know that 'my' Graham Gooch is not the same as anybody else's Graham Gooch, just as the Don Bradman of Annie's father was not 'the Don' that belonged to others. Think, for example, of the Australian captain Mark Taylor who declared when he was on 334 not out when playing against Pakistan in 1998. Three hundred and thirty-four not out overnight, Taylor declared the innings which meant both that his team had three days to bowl Pakistan out twice – and that he would share, not surpass, the record for highest Test score by an Australian with Don Bradman.[3]

'My' Graham Gooch is inextricably linked to my own departure from South Africa. The echoes of our politics lay thick over the ground that summer of 1984 when I first went to Lord's. The team I was watching was completely different from the one I had seen from the branch of a tree at Newlands Station in Cape Town. All the West Indian players who took part in the 1983 rebel tour of South Africa had been banned for life. The team that came to play England were all untainted. Some had had public offers and publicly refused. Others, I imagine, had been 'sounded out' in the way of these things and would have indicated their reluctance. At which point nothing more would have been said. They would have moved seamlessly, ruthlessly, from the potential inner circle to the outer circle and the subject would never have been mentioned again. Of those who went – those who remained

[3] Matthew Hayden has since surpassed this. He made 380 against Zimbabwe in Perth in 2003

in the circle – many suffered personal and political isolation for years afterwards. It wasn't quite the same for the English players. All the 'rebels' were given three-year bans, and one of them was Graham Gooch. But it was clear that the English establishment was going to be more forgiving than their West Indian counterparts. Of that touring party, in addition to Gooch, John Emburey and Wayne Larkin returned to the England fold. But not yet. For the moment they were out in the cold and in their absence a new team had coalesced around the elegant young captain, David Gower. And at Lord's in the summer of 1984 everyone was too polite to mention where Allan Lamb came from or that he was the happy beneficiary of the rebel tour. He made his Test debut at that very ground against India in 1982 just as Gooch *et al* were beginning their period of exile from the international game. They had left a gap – and someone had to fill it. And who better than the boy from Greenpoint? And what irony that the rebel place should be taken by the immigrant son from Cape Town.

It is very hard to hit the ground running in the appreciation of cricket. A sport so rich in history, in literature, in documentation – try Wisden for a start – takes some investment. You need to understand its history to appreciate its present. And I didn't really have the information at my fingertips. I couldn't do an instant potted biography of Graham Gooch. I could tell him what I knew – but it wasn't much. Gooch was a right-handed batsman and he had been around for ever. He used to take a low guard but in later years he stood very upright to face the bowlers. He had made a shedload of first-class runs in his career, some unbelievable number, fifty or sixty thousand in total. And he made the third highest Test score by an England player: 333 against India at Lord's in 1990.

I hadn't been at Lord's for the 333, but I did know that England won the match comfortably. And I also knew that in addition to Gooch's score, both Allan Lamb and Robin Smith made centuries in England's total of 653 for four declared. No one remembers that now. I only know because I was in South Africa at the time and both Lamb and Smith were South Africans who had qualified for England. And so the South African press made as much of their centuries as it did of Gooch's mammoth score. Even though Gooch went on to make another century in the second innings – an unbelievable total of 457 for the match. It remains the record for the most runs scored by a single batsman in one Test match, notwithstanding Brian Lara's single innings record of 400 not out against England in 2004.

So I knew that the question of 'who was Gooch' was not really about Graham Gooch at all. It was a question of how to understand cricket. When we consider the game, what are we talking about? Or whom? It could have been any name from any generation. Who was Pietersen, they will ask in twenty years' time? Who was Vaughan? Who were Gower, Gooch and Gatting? Who was Boycott? Who was Hammond, who was Edrich, who was Larwood? Who was Grace? And is there an answer? If there is, it was not one that came readily to mind that day. In retrospect the fantasy conversation runs like this:

'They were just men who found their best expression on green grass beneath a painter's sky. They were people like you and me, only for a time, when they were young, they sailed closer to the wind than we ever will. They were sons and fathers, they were friends and lovers, but whether by chance or design, whether by labour or by fortune, they had a talent. A pointless, glorious, incomparable talent. They found heaven on earth while we watched.'

Who, he might have asked, was Sobers? C. L. R. James had the answer – but for that he had to resort to Shakespeare:

Why, man, he doth bestride the narrow world
Like a Colossus; and we petty men
Walk under his huge legs, and peep about
To find ourselves dishonourable graves.

But aware of the jealousy in Cassius's speech, James went on to qualify it by quoting Hazlitt: 'Greatness is great power, producing great effects. It is not enough that man has power in himself, he must show it to all the world in a manner that cannot be hid or gainsaid.'

I'm not sure I would have agreed. It is the beauty of cricket – of all sport, but especially of cricket – that all its brilliance, all its magnificence, all its glory is constrained within a field that is essentially trivial. James disagrees. For him a Test cricketer – at least a West Indian Test cricketer – is the summation of a nation's history and its character. 'I cannot think seriously of Garfield Sobers without thinking of Clifford Goodman, Percy Goodman, H. B. G. Austin (always H. B. G. Austin), Bertie Harragin and others 'too numerous to mention' (though not very numerous). They systematically built up the game, played inter-island matches, invited English teams to the West Indies year after year, went to England twice before World War 1... the result of that consummation is Garfield Sobers. There is embodied in him the whole history of the British West Indies. Barbados has established a tradition that today is the strength not only of Barbados but of the West Indian people...'

And what would one have said of Gooch? That he was the summation of the history of the English people? Perhaps only if we go on to consider what James says next: 'But if there is the national strength, here is also the national weakness.' In the case of the West Indies, this weakness was its inability to provide a living for its talent. People like Sobers had to earn their crust abroad and, specifically, in England. How ironic, then, that Gooch sought his fortune at apartheid's dismal door. Was he, as James said of Sobers, 'one of us'? Were we 'some of him'? I suspect, properly, the answer is yes. Graham Gooch and his decision to tour can only properly be understood if we think of him, as Hugo Young later said of Margaret Thatcher, as 'one of us'.

The real conversation was more prosaic.

'He could bat,' I said. 'He could really bat. When he hit the ball from the middle, it stayed hit.' And perhaps he knew that I meant the middle of the pitch and the middle of his bat and the middle of his heart.

But who needs words when there's a bat to make? It takes shape slowly, like a flower. The kitchen table is the soil and the sandpaper is the water. The stem emerges from the rough-hewn cleft. Its leaves take shape against a backdrop of wood shavings. They fall like early petals to our tiled floor. The flower itself is made by hand. We shape the back experimentally and in stages. Sometimes a week passes and nothing happens. Other days, when the weather is good, we sit in the garden and work at it slowly. It is the mirror image of the boy's broken metatarsal. As the bone grows, the bat shrinks. We shave off pieces on one side and have to balance them on the other. We sand it all by hand until it is smooth like ice. The hardest part is to give the blade, the front of the bat, a slightly concave bow.

My daughter watches us from the corner of one eye, mollified only slightly that her plans for the summer have not been completely disrupted. They still get about. He still comes to visit. His foot is recovering faster than expected. For all my efforts his interest in cricket is sporadic and partial. Secretly my daughter is glad. She feels him returning to her, not that he has ever really been away. They're so much a couple now that my son teases them for being married. They're so confident in their love they laugh it off. They hold hands on the sofa. When it's their turn to wash the dishes they make it a game. He splashes her. She splashes back. We leave them to it.

And I work on the bat. He is more in the consultant role. He looks along the edge and sucks his teeth. He talks knowledgeably about balance and 'spring'. I tell him it's not a skateboard. He pretends not to have heard. Do we have a design in mind? Not that I know of. The law of cricket provides for the proper dimensions for a bat. Or rather, for the maximum sizes allowed: 'The bat overall shall not be more than 38 inches/96.5 cm in length. The blade of the bat shall be made solely of wood and shall not exceed 4¹/4 inches/10.8 cm at the widest part.' Other than that you're free to make what you will. We make something big and solid and a little unwieldy. We make a bat for a giant and we use it like midgets. We know we should take more off, but we are afraid. Take too much off one side and you have to match it on the other. And once it's off, there's no going back.

'We should leave it like it is,' he says.

'Okay,' I say.

'I mean, it's been fun.'

'Yes.'

'But it would be a risk to do more.'

It's the India Test at Lord's in a couple of weeks. This should be much more interesting than the West Indians. A sterner test, and several genuine stars of the game. I'm looking forward to it immensely. I was at Lord's in 1996 when Ganguly made his debut and scored a century in the process. Tendulkar, by that time, was an 'old hand' even though he was only 23 years old. This time there are a couple of other survivors from the 1996 team. Dravid (now captain) and Kumble. What a line-up!

'Do you want to go?' I ask. I'm sure I can rustle up some tickets from somewhere.

'No, not really,' he says.

A risk, I guess, to do more.

I LOVE…

That James Bond never played cricket

But still, I would like to give it one more go. Maybe later when the one-day series against India begins. Trouble is, we'll be away for much of it. Our holidays this year are taking us to France.

'Um,' says my daughter.

Where have I heard this before?

'You know we're going to France for our holidays?'

I do.

'Um…' she says. 'The house we've got… I mean… is it… I mean how many people…?'

I'm in a generous mood. And besides, I quite like the boy. We've got used to each other. We've got used to our silences. We've made a bat together.

'There's plenty of space,' I say. 'He just has to organise his own flight.'

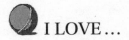

No need to ask who 'he' is. But some need to think about arrangements. In truth I am not very sure about what accommodation we have organised for the summer. It sounds idyllic, a place in Provence. But the only description we have is from a website and you never quite know what you're getting until you're there. But it will easily sleep 'ten or more' and so what is one more boy? If worst comes to worst, he can sleep on the veranda.

'Thanks, Daddy,' she says. 'I love you.'

'We'll need to rent a bigger car,' says my girlfriend, 'if there's going to be six of us.'

In fact there will be more than that. Some friends are coming to join us from Canada. Others might or might not appear. It should be fun.

'Just think,' says my girlfriend. 'Three weeks with no cricket.'

'Cool,' says my daughter.

'I'll be walking properly,' says her boy.

My daughter covers his hand with hers and smiles at a private thought.

The week before we go I endure a miserable cup game somewhere in the wilds beyond London's North Circular Road. Chasing 208 to win, we are all out for 174. A truly pathetic performance. Flat pitch, lousy opposition. Everyone – and no one more than me – got themselves out trying to hit the ball too hard. We didn't even use up all our 40 overs. My contribution to this was three runs off the edge and clean bowled trying to put the third ball I faced into orbit. Oh, and I dropped a catch for good measure. The trouble with cup games is they *are* about winning. Lose and you're out, it's that simple. Win and you're through. And we lost and we're out.

Fortunately I am old and wise now. These things no longer depress me. I take them in my stride. I'm just glad to be out in the middle with the scent of mown grass in my nostrils and the tickle of hayfever in my eyes.

And if you believe that you'll believe anything. So, alright, I admit it. I am a little grumpy. But still, when I get home the sun is shining. There is food on the table and laughter in the air. I sit outside on the bench and begin to work at the bat again. A local joiner – a fellow cricket enthusiast – has cut the splice for us. It fits perfectly; you almost don't need the glue. I have to even up the handle before we bind it with string. Almost done, now. A perfect cricket bat. A little heavy, perhaps; the weight a little too low. But for a mid-wicket specialist? Perfect. Connect with that bat and you're never going to get caught on the boundary. No matter how big the field.

But first we have to finish the handle. And knock in the bat. And oil it. 'Knocking in' is most important. It serves to compress the wood grain at the front – to make it strong – and to leave the grain at the bag 'loose', which is what gives a bat power and 'spring'. It's a lonely way to spend your time. The incessant knocking drives everyone else away, but it's not without its therapeutic value. The rhythmic clonk of wood on wood has a certain visceral appeal and takes away from the disappointments of the day's cricket.

They leave me to it. When a few minutes later I go through to the front of the house, I find they've turned the living room into a cinema. Curtains closed against the summer evening light. Lights dimmed. Bowls overflowing with popcorn. Cushions stacked up for extra comfort. My daughter even tells everyone to turn their mobiles off. She and her boy form a shapeless, inseparable blob on the sofa… They're watching the latest James Bond movie, newly out on DVD.

I'm watching them as the familiar theme music swells. I think of asking them to turn it down, but don't. I recall the time I produced a film about the making of a James Bond film. On our first shooting day there were grey clouds over Pinewood and the air smelled of arc lights and bacon sandwiches. At one point we found ourselves filming a film crew filming a film crew. One of those slightly ridiculous experiences where you imagine yourself in a lift filled with mirrors and watch ever-receding images of yourself as you disappear into insignificance. Bright lights all around and nothing to show for them. 'All experience is an arch,' said Tennyson on behalf of his hero, Ulysses, 'wherethro' / Gleams that untravel'd world whose margin fades / Forever and ever as I move.' No untravelled world gleamed on that wet day at the studios. Bond films may not all be the same, but they feel that way to me.

Despite the pyrotechnics, a film about the making of James Bond remains very much within the bounds of human thought. Not even close to the boundary. In cricket terms you would say it hardly gets off the pitch. Certainly there are 'no runs there'. Our film was aimed at students and so we were much concerned with the theory of film. Of narrative arcs and the three acts. Of beginnings, middles and endings. Of continuity. The director gave us an interview in which he said how important it was that everything made sense. It was hard to disagree and out of politeness – or expedience – we expressed no view on whether he achieved this particular end. Do James Bond films make sense? Answers on a postcard please. Instead we moved on to speak about the other requirements of film. Of the need for a love interest. Of the need for Bond to have the latest weapons. And, to a degree, of the morality or otherwise of vigilante espionage. I remember standing at Pinewood and joking with one of the crew members.

'Same old, same old,' he said with the amiable weariness accessible only to the more highly paid members of his profession.

'Who wins?' I asked.

'I haven't read the whole script,' he said. 'But I'm guessing Bond.'

It's not just Lord's. I also go to play my cricket matches on my motorbike. I have a kit bag that just about stays within the limits of what you're allowed to put on the back of a motorbike. It makes me look a little like those people you see setting off to cross Africa, with spare petrol cans hanging off the tank and a great mound of equipment in the oversized panniers. But still, it works. And it means I don't have to hang around afterwards and wait for the drinkers to have a pint or three before hitching a lift back to the club. So I usually get home reasonably quickly, even if I sometimes struggle to get out of third gear on account of the cramp in my toes. Today the journey home was quick, easy and a bit chilly. It is a little before seven. The boy's crutches are in the hallway. He no longer needs them, and somehow they have stayed at our house rather than anywhere else. I have a sudden memory of the first time I brought him home from Lord's. The way he took his helmet off and shook his hair loose like someone in a shampoo commercial. You know, one of those ones where the actor is sitting (implausibly, I always felt) in a glade in paradise washing their hair. At the appropriate moment the actor – or, more likely, actress – flicks her newly washed hair so that the drops of soapy water catch the convenient back-lighting from the sun that has chosen that moment to set between the palm fronds. In our hallway the boy's hair settled back and obscured his eyes. My daughter reached out to move it and looked into them. They managed not to kiss each other, but the eagle-eyed amongst us (me, my son, my girlfriend) noticed the soft brushing of hands and their shy smiles of delight.

'So,' said my girlfriend. 'Who won?'

She probably meant the cricket.

'Me,' I said.

'Him,' said the boy. We all looked at him. 'Joke,' he said, which is the prerogative of winners everywhere.

As I knock in the bat in the back garden, I listen to the radio reports of the day's proceedings at Lord's. The first Test against India. As always the Indian team had arrived in the midst of much hype. Their batting line-up – Tendulkar, Dravid, Ganguly and the rest – is certainly impressive. There is much talk that this might be Tendulkar's last series in England. The 'little master' has been at it for twenty years. Who knows whether he will be back? But he has never made a hundred at Lord's. No mention on the honours board. And this time he fails again. In the first innings he was out, LBW to Anderson, for 37. Today he has 'failed' again. (I wish I got sixteen when I failed.) He is out, LBW to Panesar for sixteen. His match is over. Overall it's been a hard-fought contest and at the end of the fourth day it looks as if England are in a position to force a victory. At close of play India are 137 for three. They're chasing a total of 379. Very high – nobody says impossible these days – for a fourth innings chase. My girlfriend brings me tea. She smiles briefly at the radio – the constant companion to her life – and hesitates. She can't resist asking.

'Who's winning?' she says.

If there is one question which, more than any other, simultaneously displays ignorance of the game of cricket and ties up the person being asked in impotent stuttering, it is 'Who's winning?' Because the answer is... no one. It is the nature of the game that you cannot ever, definitely, say who is winning. At least not in Test cricket. In Twenty20 you can. I went to a match at the Oval the other day. Surrey v. Essex. It was all over in the first three overs when Surrey had lost three wickets for ten runs. From then on, no matter how hard they tried, they were never in the game. But Twenty20 is different and – not as I write, anyway – not really cricket. It is a new game and we shouldn't be confused by the fact that it is played on the same fields by the same people. In Twenty20 you can ask 'Who's winning?' and expect a sensible answer. In Test cricket, you can't.

In every other sport, someone will be ahead. In cricket you may have the advantage – but you are not winning. Your lead may be unassailable and their position may be hopeless, but you are not winning. The balance is merely in your favour. And they are not losing, although 'things may not look good'. But how to explain this? Even in tennis and other sports, which do not depend on time, it is possible to say someone is winning. He may or may not win in the end, but you can point to one or other player and say at this moment, he is winning. He is ahead. Not so in cricket.

At Lord's, that day I first took the boy wonder, there had been an American in the row in front of us. He was with an English guy. Business colleagues, I guess, although they sounded like they knew each other better than that. Maybe they were at university together. The American was older and regarded himself as wiser. The Englishman was trying to bury himself in the cricket, but the truth was there was not much happening. The session between lunch and tea was not the kind of cricket in which you can bury yourself. It was the kind of cricket during which your eye strays to the tabloid newspaper left on the seat beside you by the guy who has gone in search of his bookie or the pub. Or most likely both.

'Who's winning?' asks the boy.

'Good question,' says the American. The boy nods in agreement. The English guy and I look at each other.

'No one,' we say in unison. It's the oldest conversation in the book. I've had it a hundred times. With my girlfriend, with foreigners, with Americans.

'Five days and no one wins?' they say.

'Yes.'

There is invariably a pause.

'That's the beauty of it,' I say.

'You guys are crazy.'

Well, yes. Up to a point.

'It was only day one,' I said to my girlfriend at supper that night. Like her, I was probably talking about the cricket. 'There's a long way to go yet.'

'Four more days,' said the boy. He *had* been paying attention.

My daughter rolled her eyes. 'You're not going again, are you?'

The boy hesitated. My heart sang.

'No,' he said. He looked down at his plate. He had to go home anyway.

'Did you enjoy it?' my girlfriend had asked. A mistake. The direct question is too much of a threat. The danger of a follow-up (Why? How? What exactly?) is too great. He doesn't answer. He has a sudden and obsessive interest in his shoes.

The others take a break from their Bond movie. Time for refills of popcorn and other nutrient-free foodstuffs.

The boy hears the radio as well. Aggers chatting amiably about the 'little master'.

'Who's winning?' he asks. Like I have taught him nothing.

It's time for one of my fantasy answers. If only I wasn't so tired.

'The reason cricket is the greatest sport ever invented,' I say, 'the reason it represents the high point of Western and other civilisations, the reason we can legitimately claim that 10,000 years of unremitting progress since the last ice age has led us to the point where fifteen men (I'm counting the batsmen and the umpires) can stand in a field and watch a ball go by and still believe themselves reasonable, is this: cricket is art. And this is also the reason you cannot – should not – ask the question about winning. To ask who's winning is fundamentally to misunderstand the nature of the thing.

'What kind of art, you say? I'll tell you. You've got to think of it like a novel. A game of cricket is a story. And a Test match is a great story. Think of *Moby Dick*. Think of *War and Peace*. Think of the *Heart of* bloody *Darkness*. You don't read *Moby Dick* and say, "Who won?"'

'I've never read them,' says my daughter. It occurs to me that the boy too may never have read *Moby Dick*. Or any of them. I mean, if he can get through school without playing cricket, he can surely manage without the Great Tradition? Austen, Eliot, Conrad, Lawrence. The whole lot of them out the window. It's to be expected, I suppose. I needed to cut my Achilles tendon before I got interested in any book that didn't have pictures. And even then I started on the pulp end of the 'classics' market. Buchan and Scott. Kipling and Wilkie Collins. *Stalky and Co.* was an absolute favourite. To be read and reread while I spent that long summer plotting revenge on innumerable enemies. The books I read were the sort of books you could find on my parents' shelves. Leftovers from their childhoods. Gifts from their parents or aunts or uncles.

Maybe mine will start reading the Bond oeuvre. The inspirational effect of cinema. Getting kids to read again.

'It's the same with cricket. You're watching a story unfold.'

The boy is keeping up. He honestly is. After a fashion.

'Is that the one about the whale?' he asks.

It is. *Moby Dick,* I mean. Not *Casino Royale. Casino Royale* is about a dinosaur.

'I saw something on TV. The whale won.'

There is, I suppose, a sense in which the whale can be judged to have won although I can imagine a hundred undergraduate essays speculating on the price of victory. Mind you, he did better than Ahab. If you're looking for a winner in *Moby Dick*, I would have thought that Ishmael's your man. One of the quiet ones for whom it is obvious that to survive is to win. Like Rousseau in the French revolution. Or was it Voltaire? You find them in cricket too. Not Boycott, for whom survival as a batsman was an article of faith. He was too good for that. His survival was only the beginning. But someone like Andrew Strauss, say. Or Graham Thorpe. Men who can make a century without ever playing a memorable shot. Men whose wagon wheel is almost completely devoid of boundaries and by contrast have lots and lots of ones and twos accumulated behind the wicket. On both sides. Nudgers and nurdlers. But how they get their runs is secondary. The main point about them is that they are survivors. They do not give their wicket cheaply. They do not take great risks. They do not fight great white whales in the southern oceans. They do not pursue their dreams beyond the bounds of human thought. They are practical people. Useful people. Successful people. I am vaguely comforted by this thought.

Or Starbuck. I guess he was a winner. But I find this less comforting.

'Yes,' I say, 'but when you've finished reading it, that's not what you ask. You don't say, "Who won?" It's the same with cricket. Cricket is about the battle between bat and ball, about the ebb and flow of fortune, about character and plot. It is about the middle, not the ending.'

'Like James Bond,' says my daughter. 'People think he always wins but he doesn't.'

My girlfriend and I exchange glances.

'Because he's in love with the girl, right? But she betrays him and she kills herself. I mean, is that winning?'

'But he beat *Le* whatsit,' says the boy. 'And he was never in love with her. He just...'

Obviously the subject of what Bond 'just...' is not suitable for a family discussion. A result! The boy's eyes stray to the picture on the wall. My daughter blushes.

'It doesn't matter who won. What matters is the journey. Intellectual, emotional, whatever. What matters is how you experience it.'

'Are we done?' says my son, 'cos I'd like to experience some more popcorn.'

I LOVE…

Playing away

'Um, Dad?' says my daughter. It's late June. Maybe early July. The early summer rains have finally, temporarily abated. It's a glorious day. Sunshine everywhere. The world outside our window has the kind of verdant sheen that hurts my eyes. The sky is the deep blue not of England, but of the Karoo. It is reflected in my daughter's eyes, or perhaps it is the other way round.

'Uh, you busy?'

I'm not. But you know that by now.

'There's something I wanted to ask.'

'Oh, okay.' I look past her shoulder to where I have come to expect her boy to be. There is no sign of him.

'It's just that, you know we're going to this gig tonight?'

'I do.'

'And you know it's in… well, you know he lives… what I mean is…?'

Of course we knew it was coming. Before even I bought the bed, the one with the nice veneer and the study legs. From the start the pattern has been that he came to ours. When he slept over it was at ours. When they went to gigs it was me that hung around on the pavement sometime after midnight with lots of other middle-class parents. Let's say it was the Brixton Academy. And let's say a sub-heavy metal band was playing sub-heavy metal music. And let's assume that the weather has taken a sudden turn for the worse. You'd think it was February rather than late May. Unless of course you were at Lord's, in which case you would regard this as par for the course. The rain slants in at 45 degrees. A cold wind sweeps down Stockwell Road. You can smell the rotting stench of the not-so-distant Thames on its breath. Which is just as well, because it partially disguises the sweet aroma of skunk and what I believe the Home Secretary refers to as 'other cannabis derivatives' that hangs in a cloud on the groups of young (and not so young) men who from time to time will sidle up to me or any of the other unhappy, huddled parents waiting for their offspring.

'Skunk, skunk,' they say. 'Good skunk, good skunk.' Like they're calling for their dog, Skunk, who they've inadvertently mislaid on a late-night London street. I imagine Skunk as some kind of collie cross-breed. All wagging tale and enthusiastic panting. The dealers call for her – her? – the way I might call for my daughter if she doesn't make an appearance soon. We parents decline what turns out to be an offer of drugs and shrug ourselves deeper into the inadequate coats we have brought on the assumption that we would be able to stay in our cars. One of several mistakes we have made. We were also wrong to think that the gig would end on time. Or that we would find parking. Or that immediately it was over the young people would come to the place we agreed to meet them. When, eventually, they emerge from the building it is with glazed eyes and glistening skin.

And when they were doing nothing in particular, when they were watching TV or eating or simply hanging out, they did it at ours. Or on the Heath which (again, you know) I regard as mine. So it amounts to the same thing.

Similarly it fell to us to guide our daughter and the boy wonder in the paths of culture. Early visits to the galleries and museums of London have not been a great success, but after a few weeks we have a breakthrough. I don't know what it is about Hogarth, but he appeals. 'Marriage A-la-Mode: The Tête à Tête' strikes a chord with the young man.

'I like that,' he says. 'I really like that.'

My girlfriend silences me with a glance. I do not ask how or why or what. I stand and nod slowly and admire, pretending for all the world that I like it too.

My daughter looks worried.

'Why?' she asks. 'It looks horrible.'

She doesn't mean the painting. She means the characters. She means the social narrative. She means the sight of a marriage bathed in dissolution and swaddled in misery. She means the kind of life she doesn't want to have. She is holding his hand. She lets it go in case he doesn't get the answer right.

'But it's funny,' he says. 'He's having a laugh.'

'They're not,' says my daughter. 'Not the people in the picture.'

Which, naturally, is where she has put herself.

All of which passes through my mind as she works herself round to the inevitable question.

'Dad?'

'Yes?'

'I was wondering… would it be alright if I stayed at his after the concert?'

Oh, that.

*

My girlfriend and I toss a coin and I lose. I will have to go and meet his father. His parents divorced a while ago. His mum has a new family and he now lives with his dad.

'What will we talk about?' I ask.

My girlfriend is unsympathetic.

'It's time for some payback from all that cricket,' she says.

Whatever can she mean?

'What am I looking for?'

But my girlfriend has found some urgent business elsewhere. I will have to handle this myself.

I play cricket in one of the lower divisions of one of the lesser Middlesex leagues. Every Saturday I climb on my motorbike and head off into the wilderness of north London. It is one of the curiosities of the English county game – and the English counties – that Middlesex doesn't exist. It is a figment of people's imagination. A mythical place where people play cricket and rugby, but that's all. I can list the places; they sound like the kind of suburbs of London of which *Private Eye* likes to make fun. Neasden, Kenton. Hanwell, Sudbury. Places beyond London's pale which, in my view, means anything outside Zone 2.

These journeys have a kind of metaphysical aspect for me. The rest of the team gather at the club and throw their kit into the car of whichever poor unfortunate has volunteered to drive that day. My routine is different. I go direct from home, and I go alone. It's my favourite moment of the day, possibly of the week. It is the moment at which I abandon any pretence of responsibility. For the other 160 hours of the week I am the very model of modern manhood. I wash and cook. I do homework and arrange dentists. I am there when the kids need me and I stay home when my girlfriend is busy. I don't go to the pub or the dogs or the betting shop or any of the other myriad distractions on offer. I am family man personified.

Except from midday on Saturdays in summer. At midday on Saturdays, I pull on my helmet, strap my kit on to the bike and head off down the road. And for the next eight hours the rest of the world might as well not exist. I have said elsewhere that I can lose myself in thoughts of Collingwood's catch or Pietersen's reverse sweep, but if you really want to watch the world wash from my shoulders, midday on Saturday is the time to do it.

My girlfriend is very understanding. She even likes it when I have away games. It means she is under no obligation to come and watch. Not that she comes to home games either.

'It's really not necessary,' says my daughter.

'Yes, but…' I say. At my most persuasive again. My daughter knows it's a lost cause. Ever since she was little, we've insisted on meeting the parents of friends before sleepovers.

'Oh, for heaven's sake,' she says. 'It's not a sleepover.'

Well, technically…

She's not in the mood for technicalities. Her blue eyes flash like diamonds in the night.

'I'm not a girl anymore.'

She has a point, but I'm not about to concede it.

'I know, sweetie…'

She looks at her boy. He shrugs.

'Say something,' she says. (Interesting tactic. I wonder if it will work if I try it. I resolve to, next time he says, 'Yeah, alright.')

'Dad's cool,' says her boy. 'He can't believe you got me to go to cricket.'

'I can't believe you broke his foot,' says my daughter. She

really should have moved on by now. After all, the boy is walking freely again, although not, I notice, spending any time on his skateboard.

Away changing rooms vary from really quite nice (meaning, in a public school somewhere on the outskirts of London) to the truly abysmal. There's one in a field just where the final suburb dies and the cows begin that resembles nothing so much as a Great War foxhole. Complete with rubble, the smell of something suspiciously like gas and the bodies of the dead. The dead are only rats, but they don't half add to the effect. That and the rubble and brick on the floor where the north-east corner of the room has collapsed in on itself. The smell of gas comes from an old boiler. It too has collapsed in on itself. It may or may not be connected to a live main. Half the team opt to change outside. The rest of us squash into the dirty, smelly room and change. We trip on each other's shoes. We tie our shoelaces and look up to find someone else's backside only inches from our noses as they struggle to pull on their whites. We look around for hooks to hang our clothes and end up stuffing our shirts and trousers and jackets into our kit bags. And, eventually, blinking, emerge into the sunlight.

I need a pretext. His foot provides one. The bat another.

'Come, on,' I say one evening. 'I'll give you a ride home.'

'Are you sure?'

I am.

'We can take your crutches back. Now that you don't need them.'

'Well, thanks very much.' He's running his hand down the spine of the bat. For the first time I notice what delicate hands he has. Long, thin, strong-looking hands. Young hands. Hands that have not spent their summer rubbing spit into old leather. Hands without calluses. Soft hands. A lover's hands.

Some thoughts are best left unsaid. I indicate the bat.

'Did you tell your dad about it?'

He did. He pauses.

'We could take it and show him,' I say. My second pretext, but he turns it down. 'Cricket's not his thing,' he says. 'And it's not really my bat.'

It's beginning to rain and so we go by car.

'Your dad doesn't play?' I ask.

The boy shakes his head.

'Rugby.'

Ah. Rugby. A one-word rebuttal of everything to do with cricket. Of course it is perfectly possible to play both rugby and cricket, to watch both rugby and cricket. To enjoy both games. But I understand what the boy means. There are some people who like all sports. And there are some who like one sport. His father clearly belongs to the latter group.

They live in a house much like ours at the end of a train line. I lift my hand to ring the bell, but the boy has his keys out.

'Dad!' he calls. 'Dad? There's someone you should meet.'

Which is what my daughter said the first time the boy loomed tall in our hallway.

We shake hands. He offers me a drink. I wonder what on earth to say.

'So,' he says, 'you've come to check us out?'

I'm about to protest, but he shrugs. 'You're right to do it,' he says. 'I should have checked you out too, but you know... I only have boys. It's different with girls.'

Well, maybe it is. I don't know. They offer me a tour of the house, but I decline.

'I just wanted to say hello. After all, we're stealing your son for the summer.'

It's been decided he is coming with us to France.

'Oh, yes, thank you.'

There is a silence. One of those delicate moments when everyone sips their tea and looks at the floor.

'So cricket?' he says.

'Yes.'

It is the great conundrum of cricket. You score runs by hitting the ball. Very often you get out by hitting the ball. Or by trying to hit the ball when you would have been better off having nothing to do with it. It's one of the hardest things to teach eleven- and twelve-year-olds. They see a cricket ball coming at them and they want to hit it. But many balls are best left unhit. Watch someone like Neil McKenzie, the South African batsman. In the Lord's Test of 2008 he left ball after ball after ball. Jimmy Anderson bowled well, but with virtually no reward. Why? Because the batsmen wouldn't play the ball. 'You've got to make them play,' Geoffrey Boycott said on the *TMS* commentary. 'You've got to make them play.' He can't say it often enough. Cricket is a contest between bat and ball. If the pitch is too easy, it makes it unfair on the bowlers. If the pitch is uneven, the advantage moves to the bowler. Either way, if the batsman doesn't have to play, if he doesn't have to protect his wicket, there is no real contest. So bowlers can use the full range of weapons in their armoury. They can bounce and short and seam and move. But in the end, the balls that get batsmen out are the ones they have to play at. And batsmen who don't want to get out should leave as many balls alone as possible.

The boy leaves us alone.

'I must just go and...'

He doesn't say what. Text my daughter, perhaps. His father and I look at each other.

'It's lasted longer than I thought,' I say.

He nods. 'A lot longer.' Then a sudden chuckle. 'Christ, almost longer than my marriage.'

I smile the understanding smile of a man who has never married. Not in so many words. Even though my girlfriend and I are about to celebrate our twentieth anniversary.

'She's his first,' he says. I hope he means girlfriend.

'For her too.'

'They seem happy.'

'Yes.'

I saw a film once of Bob Woolmer coaching kids on how to leave a ball. What happens is the bowler bowls. The batsman goes forward to play it. At the last moment he realises the ball is

a) too good, and
b) not going to hit the stumps.

So it is better to leave it. He pulls his bat inside the line of the ball and it goes through to the keeper. But he has to do it quickly, otherwise the ball will catch the edge of the bat and be caught by the keeper or the slips.

'Are they...?' he asks. ' I mean, is she...? How old is... is she sixteen yet?'

She is. He nods. I nod. We drink some tea. Neither of us wants to go anywhere near the ball.

'Well, nice to meet you,' I say.

'Yeah, alright,' he says.

When I get home my daughter is packing her bag for France. Her hair is newly cut. Her clothes are freshly ironed. She looks radiant and – what's the word. Beautiful.

I LOVE…

Le grillon

You haven't met Laure, but then nor had I. There's no reason you should have. But we know she exists. She lives in a small village in Provence and in my mind she wanders through sun-dappled fields wearing a sundress and smelling of lavender. She is about 28, with blue-grey eyes, a ready smile and a generosity of spirit. She could have a big job in a big city but she prefers the simple life of rural France, where she paints, writes and spends her spare time helping out at the local *école de musique*. She is naturally (but inexplicably) single.

Or perhaps not. Perhaps she is an 84-year-old toothless crone recently released from serving a twelve-year stretch for murdering her two sisters. Not having met her, it's hard to tell.

What we do know about Laure is that she is part of the information superhighway. She has broadband internet access and a Wi-Fi transmitter and she lives just off the main square of the village to which we have decamped for the summer holiday. She also has failed to put any password protection on her Wi-Fi – which is why I think of her as having a generosity of spirit but which doesn't quite explain why I think of her as 28, pretty and as having blue-grey eyes. She is, nevertheless, my point of access to the outside world. Unbeknownst to her, I can sit at the cafe nursing my café au lait and surf the net via her Wi-Fi broadband connection. Except I don't surf at all. What I do is keep up with the cricket.

For hours. And more or less in secret. My girlfriend thinks I am working. She thinks I have a job that requires me to be in touch with the outside world. This is – up to a point – true. I do have such a job and I do have to be in touch with the world. For ten minutes a day. It's the other four hours that are hard to explain.

It took me a while to find Laure, but once I did there is no stopping me. The waiter at the cafe is called Paul. Over the ten days we have been in Provence, Paul has grown used to my ways. He has begun to think it normal for a man to sit in the shade of a plane tree, an earpiece in one ear, transfixed by events far away. Early on he made the mistake of asking what it was I was reading.

'It is important, no?' he asked. 'I see from how your face it look.'

'*Très important*,' I agreed. Paul is trying to improve his English. I am trying to improve my French. His English is better than my French but I am less ambitious in what I try to say. The square is overlooked by a twelfth-century chapel guarded by a statue of the Virgin Mary. My eyes at that moment are fixed on her although I am not in fact seeing her. What I am seeing is the arc of the ball as Matt Prior steps down the pitch at the Rose Bowl and plonks Zaheer Khan over his head for six. How do I know? Because the scoreboard told me so. Television may have made more these days than previously of the wagon wheel diagram to show how and where a batsman scored his runs, but the staple for any record of the game is what we call 'stats', short for 'statistics', meaning, according to my Chambers at least, 'tabulated numerical facts'. This is only an approximation of what cricketing statistics mean. An understatement. It is the outline of a story. It is painting by numbers, only with more artistry. In cricket the numbers tell you everything you need to know and the astute reader of the numbers – rather like my daughter reading the lines of my face – can construct an entire story out of them. Balls bowled, runs scored, extras, overs, wickets, fours, sixes. The whole lot. If, like me, you have spent more of your life than is strictly healthy watching cricket, it is perfectly possible to watch the game on Teletext. Take, for example, the second Test in the 2008 England tour to New Zealand. We'll ignore the first Test because it was dismal beyond speech or remembering. But the second test? The second Test was wonderful. For once the England selectors used form rather than sentiment as a basis for selection. Hoggard and Harmison were dropped and in their place we got a rejuvenated James Anderson and the even more youthful Stuart Broad. England posted a reasonable total in the first innings (thanks almost entirely to a face-saving maiden Test century from Ambrose) and skittled New Zealand out for 198 in their first innings. By the time England had finished their second innings, early on day four, New Zealand needed to make what would have been a record-breaking 440-something to win. An impossible score. Even with nearly seven sessions of play remaining, and notwithstanding anything Gordon Greenidge may have managed at Lord's in 1984, it was a fantasy score. New Zealand have a few batsmen capable of accumulating big scores and they have McCullum who doesn't so much accumulate as annex, but this would be a truly heroic effort. As the opposing captain therefore, as Michael Vaughan, you know what you have to do. You surround the bat and you wait. Runs may come, but you don't care about runs, because wickets will come too. You can spend 30 or 40 runs buying each wicket. It's the cricketing equivalent of a Russian oligarch moving in on a premiership football club. Money – runs – are not the problem. And things are looking propitious. In the first innings Anderson got a five-for. In the second there is a howling gale blowing. It is likely that Sidebottom's swing will be a problem. So you bring the bowlers on and you wait for the wickets to fall.

Now I was listening to this on the radio and it became irritating. Irritating because what was there for the commentary team to say? It's not that I mind the commentators. On the contrary I am fond of all of them, even Geoffrey Boycott. Especially Geoffrey. Because he knows his stuff and he tells it as he sees it. But there was nothing they could say that would add to the drama. The stage had been set; the polite thing to do was stand back and let the drama unfold. The tension was there by default. Nothing they could say would add to or detract from the simple equation: New Zealand needed an impossible number of runs. England needed to be patient. And so did the audience. It was no good hoping for a wicket with this ball or the next one or the one after that. Cricket doesn't work like that. Cricket demands patience. And so after a while I turned the sound off. Now all I had was the BBC Interactive screen showing the score, the batsmen's names and scores and who was bowling. And as each ball went by a little figure pops up at the bottom of the screen giving how many runs were scored.

And this was more than enough. That was the point. I could imagine with great precision everything I wasn't seeing. I could picture the slip cordon for Broad and Anderson. Four of them? Five. Let's call one of them gully. Someone in the covers. Mid-off, mid-on. How many does that leave? There are nine fielders plus the bowler and the wicket keeper, so that leaves Bell at short leg for the bat-pad catch and someone down at fine leg just to show willing. For Sidebottom it would be different because most of the time he would be swinging the ball in to the batsman. So you pull one of the slips out and have someone in a catching position at square leg instead. And the batsmen? The batsmen (with the exception of McCullum, who wants to hit everything) want to let everything go by. But they can't. That's the secret to this kind of game. Geoffrey Boycott can't say it often enough. 'You've got to make them play,' he says and he's right. You have got to make them play. In cricket you score runs by playing. In cricket you get out by playing. It is the uber-allegory for us all. It is the source of all tension and all drama. And we know this. Boycott famously described it with a phrase that so bordered on the poetic that it has been repeated until it is almost meaningless. The phrase is 'the corridor of uncertainty', an imaginary line, just outside off stump, where a bowler may bowl and thereby create in the batsman's mind a sufficient degree of doubt as to whether he should play or not. The uncertainty arises because of that simple equation. If he plays it, he might get out. If he doesn't play it… he might get out. So what should he do? Remember that the batsman has something less than a second to make up his mind, but for those of us watching, it is why we follow the game. We follow it for the exquisite agony of the dilemma that is cricket: the very thing that brings you success will, sooner or later, bring your downfall. No matter who you are and no matter how good you are. Sooner or later you will get out not because you didn't play the ball but because you did. You may be caught in the five-man slip cordon or you may be caught on the boundary at mid-wicket. Or even by Ian Bell at silly short leg. It doesn't matter. What does matter is that it will be your fault. Your shot. Your choice. We know this whether we are listening or watching or, in my case, simply following the numbers. I give a little grunt when a four is scored. I nod wisely when Vaughan varies his bowling attack. I purse my lips when leg byes are added to the score. And I grunt in satisfaction when a wicket falls, especially if it is a catch to the slip cordon. Because there, especially, we know what has happened. The bowler has bowled a good line; the batsman has been unsure whether to play and the edge has carried to Ambrose or Strauss or Cook or Collingwood, who are there for that simple but deadly purpose.

But Paul thinks I am seeing the Virgin Mary. He also thinks this accounts for the look of transcendental delight on my face.

'Ah,' he says. 'You are with God.'

'*Mon Dieu*,' says Aggers on *Test Match Special* on the BBC.

'Now, now, Jonathan,' says Geoffrey Boycott. 'English only, please. This is cricket.'

I am inclined to agree with Paul. I am sitting in a French village, sipping coffee and following the cricket on the BBC website. I am with God. Or at least with my god.

'What's happening?' says the boy wonder. 'Let's have a look.'

A what? Can't he see I'm busy? And what is he doing here anyway? His presence in our lives is now complete but we are still negotiating what I would call questions of space. Like, for example, where he sleeps or how much space I need when I am following cricket while cadging internet access off an unknown (but we suspect lovely) Frenchwoman called Laure. The boy is happily oblivious to these social niceties and soon we are hunched together over my laptop, sharing headphones like schoolgirls on a bus as they listen to some unspeakable pop song on their mobile phone. Paul comes over to offer more coffee.

'He also listen to the church?' Paul asks.

It's time to come clean.

'*C'est ne pas l'église*,' I say. '*C'est...?*'

My daughter, eating ice cream at another table, whips out her pocket dictionary. She has become adept at finding *le bon mot* for every occasion.

'*Grillon*,' she says with an impish smile.

'*Grillon*,' I confirm.

'*Grillon?*' Paul asks.

'*Oui, c'est un sport Anglais.*'

'*Le grillon*, it is a sport?'

'*Oui.*'

'How do you say in English?'

'We say cricket.'

'*Vraiment?*'

'*Oui. Vraiment. Comme le grillon.*'

Other customers are competing for Paul's attention. He ignores them to give the matter some thought. Eventually he unfolds his chin from his barrel-like chest and delivers his verdict.

'Bof!' he says as he walks off, shaking his head.

At which point we are interrupted. Just as Prior clips Zaheer to mid-on where Dravid 'pockets an easy catch', bringing the score to 43 for one in the eleventh over, my girlfriend comes into view and insists that we are not in France to 'waste our time on cricket'. (Twenty years, dear reader, twenty years I have lived with her and she still unblushingly says things like 'waste time' and 'cricket' in the same breath.)

Apparently we have come to France to waste our time touring the perfumeries of Grasse.

'Um, Dad?' says my daughter.

'Yes?'

'Um, we thought we'd give the perfume thing a miss...'

'What will you do?'

'Oh, you know.'

Unfortunately I suspect I do. But it's too late now. I don't have a Bradman card left to play.

And even if I did?

'They look so happy,' says my girlfriend.

'Remind you of anyone?'

We exchange smiles and touch hands.

It is early evening before we get back to the village and the cricket match between India and England is long since finished. I sneak down to the tables outside Laure's windows to catch up on the scores. In the first one-day match England have posted a decent enough total of 288. Both Cook and Bell made one-day maiden centuries. India were never really in the chase and were eventually bowled out for 184. England are one up in the series, and all is well with the world.

I LOVE . . .

Scratch games

We're beside a sparkling lake. The sun glints off bleached rock. A soft wind sighs in the trees. The lake is fed by a cool green river. It plunges from the dry, craggy heights of the mountains above Grasse. There are pools and eddies, cataracts and waterfalls.

One of them is particularly enticing. The water has cut deeply into the rock. You can jump twenty feet into a thin channel of cold, green water. The boy goes first, a leader suddenly.

'I'd better get it right,' he says.

My daughter, normally a worrier, looks relaxed.

'I hope he doesn't hurt himself,' I say.

'He won't,' she says. 'He's much more athletic than he looks.'

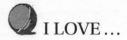

He looks pretty athletic to me, hardly like a boy at all. A few weeks in the sun and he is brown and strong. He's never going to be six-pack material, he is too tall and thin for that. But his body has filled out a little. His muscles glisten when he emerges sleekly from the water. His hair, slicked back by the water, reveals his unconventionally handsome face. In time there will be photographs of him on her wall. The ones of him leaping into the gully are particularly impressive. Taken from above they make it look even deeper and more dangerous than it was.

Now he's standing above the ravine again, peering into its dark swirling waters. He looks back to us – actually at my daughter. She nods. He raises an eyebrow. She nods again and this time he dives. The sun flashes off his back and he disappears into the cool water.

'What was he asking?'

'Well, diving's a risk,' she says.

So?

'He knows that if he gets hurt, it will mess up my holiday. Just like if I get hurt it will ruin things for him.'

It's as if they've talked about it. Perhaps I raised an eyebrow too.

'I'm good, Daddy,' she says. 'We're good. Nobody's getting hurt.'

The house we are renting is set in olive-and-fig groves against a Provencal hillside. There are wild boar in the hills above us and kestrels hover for hours on the warm thermals pushing up the mountain range to the north. The village has a *boulangerie* and a *patisserie* and not much else. It is favoured by artists and writers and others seeking the quiet life. The days are hot; the nights are warm. Sound carries for miles across the still valleys. There are a couple of restaurants off the main square and, of course, there is the *boulodrome*. In the evening it has become our habit to wander over, buy ice creams and watch the men of the village – it is always the men – play boules. To judge from the ferocity of their concentration, and from the level of vitriol (which, thankfully, I understand only partially), there is money at stake. Provencal evenings are perfect for sipping something cold and watching the *petanque*. The tension is rising. There is plenty of swearing. One of the players is Paul and his usual sunny smile has been replaced by an unwavering glower. He looks like a cartoon-strip bad guy. His bulky shoulders are hunched. His lip is bleeding slightly from where he has been chewing a toothpick. His permanent five o'clock shadow is threatening to become a beard.

'Hello, Paul,' says the boy. *'Bonsoir.'* He seems untroubled by the rising levels of ancient testosterone.

Paul ignores him. The game has reached a crucial stage. If I have been keeping score right, and judging by Paul's expression, I have, he is about to lose 13-0. This is not a good thing. There is a tradition in *petanque* that someone who loses by such a margin has to kiss 'Fanny's backside'. I don't know who Fanny is, or was, but in our village there is a small fountain with an angel and the loser has to kiss its backside. Every sport, it would seem, has its rituals of humiliation. Paul duly loses. He storms off to kiss the angel. He storms back to start another game, and it is only then that he deigns to notice us.

'Didn't go well, huh?' I say.

'Bof!' he says with a shrug. 'Maybe I give up.'

'You should play cricket,' says the boy. 'It's easier.'

'Le grillon?' Paul asks.

'Oui,' says the boy. 'I can show you. I know everything there is to know about cricket.'

'Vraiment?' says Paul.

'Vraiment?' I echo.

'Sure,' says the boy. 'I mean, *oui*.'

*

I'm surprised you even have to ask. Of course we have a ball. And a bat. And what are chairs for, if not to make wickets? And yes I know the rules say each team shall have eleven players, but I prefer to think of this as a suggestion. You're quorate with anything over four. And we had a pitch already. Anyone who has played at the Oval in late August of a hot summer will tell you it is not that different from a village *boulodrome* in Provence.

The field is quickly marked out and the teams arranged. The boy will captain one (that'll teach him) and I will captain the other. My son declines to play on the grounds this is not really cricket, but a passing ex-pat, name of Jimbo, is commandeered from his habitual seat at the bar to play on the boy's team. He also gets Paul, Paul's-underling-whose-name-I-never-got, Yelena the Serbian waitress, Jean-Pierre-the-elder and a young Australian backpacker who has got lost on the way to Draguignan. The Australian looks like he might be trouble.

'It's okay,' says his girlfriend. 'His parents were Greek.'

Which may have been true but his name was Shane, which seemed to me to owe more to the country of his birth than the heritage of his ancestors.

I get Jean-Pierre-the-younger who worked at the meat counter in the *Huit-à-huit* down the road, the Australian girlfriend (Candy), and Madame la Liseuse who teaches science in the high school in the next town but who volunteers at the tourist information centre in the evenings because she speaks about nine languages and has an encyclopaedic knowledge of all things Provencal.

'I am too old,' she says.

'Cricket is like *petanque*,' says the boy. 'You are never too old.'

I am still a couple of players short. Olivier who runs the

gallery declines on the grounds of rheumatoid arthritis and his grandson Yves is deemed too young.

'Nonsense,' I say. 'He's four.' But the French aren't having it. They have inspected the ball and know it hurts.

'There's me,' says my daughter, a fact which I have been studiously ignoring. She has many talents but catching cricket balls isn't one of them. But desperate times require desperate measures and so she joins our happy throng. They have six players. We have five. I consider myself worth two of them.

'I want to play with him,' she says. She means her boy. 'I don't want to lose.'

We'll ignore that for the moment. After some careful bartering, I acquire Shane the Australian of Greek ancestry and they get my daughter.

Game on.

The boy wins the toss and elects to field. 'I don't like the look of the pitch,' he explains. 'Uneven bounce.'

Well, yes, perhaps, but have I taught him nothing? Every captain who wins the toss and elects to field does so at his own peril. Does he not remember my moving account of the first Ashes Test of 2002? Nasser Hussain won the toss, chose to field and Matthew Hayden and Ricky Ponting proceeded to hit England's bowling attack to all parts of the field. England's fielding was dismal (Hayden was dropped three times) and Simon Jones suffered a career-threatening injury. England duly lost the match by 184 runs and Hussain's decision to field was widely blamed. Perhaps he had not studied the statistics enough. The last England captain to win the toss and elect to field in Brisbane was Len Hutton in 1954–55. Australia scored more than 600 in the first innings and won the match.

The boy doesn't care.

'Look at your batting,' he says. 'I'm backing my bowlers.'

Such bravado should not go unpunished.

'Right, I'll open,' I say. 'Me and...'

The statement becomes a question. Me and…? Shane, I'm assuming, is not great but better than most. Better save him for first wicket down or when we might need to up the run rate a little. Candy looks like she plays sport, but does she play cricket? Jean-Pierre-the younger (JPY to you and me) is a beefy bloke, but cricket requires more than brute strength. And Madame la Liseuse? Her blonde hair is neatly bobbed. She is wearing a summer dress and white sandals. Her make-up is impeccably understated. Her skin is lightly tanned. And she is smiling softly.

'I will open with you,' she says.

Which is a phrase you would only use if you have played the game before. Or watched it. Or lived with someone who loved it. Or...

I couldn't think why this provincial French schoolteacher would know anything about cricket.

'Do you want the strike?' she asks.

Well, it was only polite to say yes. I mean, it wouldn't be fair to put her in against the boy wonder who, I had no doubt, was going to open the bowling for 'them'. All through the summer he has worked on his action (and grown three inches) and he can now send down a reasonably straight, reasonably fast ball outside off stump. You don't have to fear him, but you do have to pay attention.

Except he's not going to bowl at all. He has decided to open with Paul, who approaches the crease with a murderous look on his face and the ball clutched in his meaty paw. The boy has given Paul basic instruction in the art of bowling, but the Frenchman is not interested.

'Please,' he says. 'We are in France. We do not run.'

He stands at the crease in the manner of a boules player. Both feet together, knees slightly bent, left hand waving foppishly in the breeze. A grimy cloth tucked into his waistband. I take guard. It's not clear what the tactics should be; out of politeness, if nothing else, it seems clear I should block the first ball. But the boy has an annoying grin on his face and my daughter is giggling. A judicious six should shut them all up a little.

'You are ready?' Paul asks.

I am ready. He bowls – if that's the word – a high arcing ball on off stump. He has judged the length nicely and the ball is going to land a foot in front of me. Given the pitch, it seems safer to take it as a full toss. I take a step down the pitch and swing my bat.

'Mind the windows,' says the boy just loudly enough...

...for me to hear and...

...for me to worry.

The ball lands on a pebble, shoots under my bat and hits the wicket. My son, self-appointed umpire, raises his finger and I begin what is known in the trade as the long walk back to the pavilion. I hand JPY the bat as he comes to the crease. He looks at it doubtfully, the way English people do when confronted by their first plate of steak tartare. Paul, still smarting from the defeat at boules the previous day, tosses up another ball. JPY steps forward and tries to hoick it over mid-wicket. My daughter has obviously had coaching in her sledging. *'Attendez-vouz les fenêtres,'* she says. JPY stops himself in mid shot to glare at her.

Clean bowled.

His expression changes the way an Englishman's does when the waiter breaks a raw egg over his steak tartare. For the first time in 24 hours, Paul smiles.

'*C'est facile*, no?' he says.

'*Oui*,' replies the boy wonder. '*Très facile*.'

It is time to steady the ship. I send in Shane, the Greek-Australian.

'Have a look,' I say. My homage to Rob. I refrain from telling him not to do anything stupid. Self-discipline, that's the thing.

'No worries, mate,' he says, which is always reassuring from an Aussie – as long as they're on your side.

I sit next to his girlfriend, Candy, on the low wall surrounding the *boulodrome*.

'He can play, right?'

'Not really.'

Paul, delighting in the unaccustomed freedom to move his feet (but drawing the line at actually running), takes three paces and tosses up another high one. It takes so long coming down that Shane feels he has had all the 'look' he needs. He brings the bat through from a high backlift *à la* Brian Lara and plays a perfect cover drive which, if he connects, will endanger several windows – probably in the next village.

Sadly he misses. The ball jags off a pebble, whacks him on the knee and goes through to hit the wicket.

The titters that greeted the first two dismissals become a full-scale cacophony of laughter. Half the village has turned out to watch and you don't have to know anything about cricket to know we are in bad shape. You have only to look at JPY's face. Or my daughter, who is laughing so much she can barely stand. Only Paul and the boy remain above it all. Paul is doing his Merv Hughes impression and the boy looks like Steve Waugh turning the screw on yet another hapless England batting line-up. They are huddled in conference and casting meaningful glances at Candy who, of all our batsmen, is the first to take guard. And not middle stump either. She asks for 'middle-and-leg', which you only ever do if you've played the game before.

'There are only two stumps,' says my son and Candy has to work out her guard for herself.

The fourth ball of the over. Paul, perhaps secure in the knowledge that he has his hat-trick, lets the ball stray to the leg side. Candy goes down on one knee and sweeps it for four. The next ball she drives past his left hand. Four. The sixth ball she cuts sweetly past point for four.

Easy game cricket.

Except that Madame la Liseuse is now on strike. And the boy has brought himself on to bowl. And he's bowling properly. None of this back-handed crab-claw boules nonsense for him. He takes three paces, bangs the ball in and – given the pitch is murderously hard – it rises towards Madame la Liseuse's face.

Dear God, I think, what is he doing? The same thought seems to have struck him. He has clapped his hand over his mouth like someone who realises they have just done a terrible – and irrevocable – thing. The crowd too is quiet.

Until Madame la Liseuse steps back and across her wicket (thank you, Bob Woolmer) and pulls the ball through mid-wicket for four.

'I played for my school,' she says. 'It was some time ago.'

In the interests of the boy's manhood, we shall draw a veil over the rest of that innings. Suffice it to say that sixteen balls were bowled, 47 runs were scored and Candy was run out only because she slipped on the treacherous gravel of the *boulodrome*.

Our turn.

'Presumably you bowl as well,' I say to Candy.

'No, sorry.'

'Madame la Liseuse?'

Of course she does. It's a difficult choice. Should I bowl her first or hold her in reserve? I look over to the boy's team. It's clear that he has decided to start the batting with Yelena and Jean-Pierre-the-elder. This is no time for sympathy though. We need early wickets (and they have an extra player).

'Right, I'll start,' I say. 'Shane, first change.'

The first four overs pass peacefully enough. Yelena is out trying to belt me over mid-wicket. Jean-Pierre-the-elder makes a nifty nine before being caught in the covers. Jimbo and my daughter are in. The boy is obviously holding himself in reserve for a final assault, should it be needed, and Paul has not yet recovered from his bowling exertions. They have reached 38 before another couple of wickets fall. After a couple of hotly disputed not-outs from my son, he finally raises the finger for an LBW so blatant that even my daughter goes without protest. The spirit of cricket is alive and well. Jimbo, whose fondness for the agricultural swipe is matched only by his taste for wine, is caught at mid-wicket. Paul and the boy at the crease. Ten needed to win. Madame la Liseuse to bowl. I move to field at cover point, which is the position favoured by the great athlete-fielders. Colin Bland. Jonty Rhodes. Paul Collingwood. Me.

My son knows this. He laughs. 'So which one are you?' Collingwood, since he asks.

Madame la Liseuse has a nice action but all it generates are easy off breaks. The boy turns the first one round the corner for two and drives the second for four. Four needed, one wicket required. Three balls remaining. His third shot trickles off the bat and they successfully steal a single, though only because JPY forgot which end to throw the ball to. Or, rather, he forgot which end Paul was running to. Because Paul doesn't run. He strolls in a stately manner, the way the *QE2* will edge into Southampton harbour. Still, he's on strike and there are two balls remaining. Three runs required.

'Time out,' calls the boy.

'You can't have time out in cricket,' I protest. I appeal to the umpire. 'Make them play?'

But my son watches too much American TV.

'Time out,' he says. 'Bad light.'

The brilliant Mediterranean sunlight glances off the pale buildings of Provence. The plane trees murmur in the breeze. The boy and Paul confer. I am in two minds whether it is better for us to have a team talk – or to eavesdrop on their conversation. As Yelena has been summonsed back to her job and Candy and Shane are sharing a beer, I decide to eavesdrop.

'Three?' says Paul.

'*Trois*,' the boy agrees. 'All you have to do is hit the ball to the wall.'

'The wall? *C'est facile, non?*'

'*Oui*.'

Paul contemplates the 40 yards to the wall. He looks at the setting sun. His eyes pass lazily over me.

'Bof!' he says and he walks over to take his guard.

I go over to confer with Madame la Liseuse. 'They're going for the big hit,' I say.

'I have an idea,' she says.

Instead of her normal run up, she takes a position near the stumps. Legs bent, head still, ball in hand. Her hand is held awkwardly, like a claw.

'Play,' says my son.

She flips the ball out of her hand in the manner of a boules player. It is on a decent length. Paul watches it the way a butcher might eye a rack of lamb ready for the cleaver. I am watching his bat. I see that his right hand has moved lower down the handle. I move a little closer to the wicket. He hits and catches the ball dead in the sweet spot. It screams straight at me.

'Drop it!' yells my daughter.

'Catch it!' says Candy.

Nobody suggests what I actually do, which is lose sight of it in the plane trees. It smacks me on the shoulder and turns from a window-smashing match-winner into a slow looping catch, easily held by Madame la Liseuse at the bowler's end.

Game over. We win by two runs. I go over to congratulate Madame la Liseuse.

'I never introduced myself,' she says. 'I am Laure.'

I LOVE...

The last days of the season

The young man disappears as softly as he arrived.

It's late summer for the optimists, early autumn for the pessimists. There's a chill in the air. It has crept in imperceptibly. There are wet leaves on the decking and the neighbour's ivy is a burgundy stain on their yellow grey wall. Nature's first green has become autumn's gold. The nights are shorter and the chill catches us by surprise. The season of mist is upon us. On Hampstead Heath my evening walks are quieter now. There is no longer the sound of teenagers or sport. Only the occasional dog-walker disturbs the fading light. At the men's pond the last of the summer swimmers has taken the last summer dip. The winter regulars are still there. You can hear them playing a version of badminton in the sunbathing court. Now that there is no sun. And no bathers. The ground is softer underfoot and the wind blows in from the west and sends eddies of leaves spiralling down the avenues.

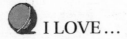

It's the same at home. In the evenings we no longer eat our supper with the door open to the garden. Our summer tans have started to fade. Dark roots appear on the heads of those of us who have hair. As if by some strange alchemy, the rack in the hall hangs heavy with the new season's coat harvest. And yet the hall is strangely empty. The cricket bags that have littered it since April have disappeared. There are no gloves drying on the radiator. There are no pads leaning against the wall. My boots and my son's boots have been stowed in the basement. The collection of old balls has been thrown out. Next season will bring new matches and new match balls. And, the match over, the balls become practice balls. And when the season is over they will be thrown out, too old and battered to be of any use. Time was when I would delight in unravelling a ball. Pick away at the stitching until the leather peels away like an orange. Unwind the string and find what's in the middle. My son still does it and from time to time I'll find a little stash of string forgotten in a drawer. The field mice that thrive in our part of north London use it for nesting.

At the club it's the weekend of the last games of the season. There is talk of annual dinners and man-of-the-season awards. A few hardy souls turn out for a damp net. I would guess that 80 per cent of us live within a two-mile radius of the club, but it is the nature of north London that we could go the rest of our lives without meeting. Were it not for cricket.

'See you around,' we say, and what we mean is that come the spring the e-mail will appear announcing a work party for the nets or the pitch or the sight screens. And a few of us will pitch up at the appointed hour. 'Yeah, alright,' we'll say, and a new season will begin.

But for the moment cricket is nearly over. The last game of the season has been cancelled. Dick and his 'boys' are relaying the pitch. Getting rid of the ridge. Only he doesn't call it that.

'It'll be perfect for next season,' he says.

I thought it always was?

'Everything needs to be refreshed from time to time.'

My daughter is back at school, starting the first year of her A-levels. She's moved school this year. There are new people and new friends. New books and new boys. New classes and a chance to do only the subjects that interest her. She talks excitedly about her teachers and the lab facilities.

It's a Thursday in September when I watch her going out the door. She and *the* boy – the old boy – went to a concert (sorry, *gig*) the night before. On the surface she looks the same. Same hair dyed black. Same old jeans. Same trainers. But something is different. She seems older somehow, as though something changed in France. More confident. More sure of herself and her place in the world. She's always had a thoughtful air; now it's as though there are thoughts to go with it. She's the last to leave. My girlfriend has gone to work; the younger children start school earlier. There's just me and the boy at the breakfast table. He has stayed over – his school starts later than hers. He is free for the day.

'So what will you do today?'

He shrugs.

'You going to get in some skateboarding?'

Another shrug.

It occurs to me that since his injury he hasn't really been skateboarding. Not in the summer before the holidays. And not at all while we were in France.

'Not interested, huh?'

He realises he has to say something.

'It's not the same,' he says. 'Not since…'

I know what he means. Some people never come back from injury. And if you do, it takes a while to regain your confidence. Some sportsmen try to hurry it – Andrew Flintoff comes to mind – and the recovery may last longer as a result. Others take the time needed – Michael Vaughan – but the pressure to perform grows with each week they're out of the game. I know the feeling too. Some seasons I 'do in' – meaning strain – my shoulder in at the first net. Pull it too hard and I know that it's 'gone' for the duration. The only way for it to recover would be for me not to play cricket. And that's not going to happen.

'You're not enjoying it as much?'

Another shrug. 'Every time I ollie I'm thinking, you know, what if…?'

'It'll come back.'

'I guess.'

We sip our tea in silence. I look at the newspaper. As always I turn to the sports pages first. He looks at the wall. A slow smile spreads on my face and his too. He knows what I'm thinking before I say it.

'You want to go to the…'

'Please,' he says. 'That would be nice.'

And not a 'yeah, alright' in sight.

Middlesex Country Cricket Club has nine home grounds and during the season they all play host to a couple of games. Lord's, of course, is the biggest and most famous, but Southgate has a special place in my heart. I've played there a few times. In the last match of the 2008 season I made 45, my top score in a rubbish year. Southgate is lovely. The church smiles across the oak trees. The hum of traffic recedes to almost nothing. There is no nicer place to fall asleep. This suburb of London was once home to rock stars and film stars. Now it slumbers gently, protected from the city by the North Circular Road. In winter the John Walker Ground plays host to football matches but the depredations of the winter game have been kept at bay by the white picket fences and hospitality tents of an end-of-season county Division 2 game against Leicestershire. The earlier match between the two teams in July ended in a draw and there is no reason to think this will be any different. But still, it'll be nice to get out. And there is some sunshine around.

London, 1 January 2002

'Can I stop now? It's exactly (well, not quite) ten years since I started writing these letters to you. It's been quite an innings. Long and slow. Not many boundaries. Not many flights of fancy. No big sixes over the bowler's head. Nothing dramatic. But I read through these pages to you and I marvel at the slow accumulation of runs. Every evening, as I recall, I would sit down to write to you. I was always tired. I never had time. How many words? How many tired nights, one eye on the television and a cup of tea balanced precariously on the arm of the sofa? But somehow I wrote, and somehow the innings grew. It's big now, a whole book almost. It's hard to tell how big it is because I've done it all by hand. Normally – but you know this – I am an impatient man. I like to get on with it. I like to hurry things along. But with you, with all of you, I can sit and wait for the long term and enjoy the waiting. And now I like to pretend these letters are about you and I know this isn't true. They always were by me, for me, about me. An indulgence, I suppose. I love these little stories, but I know that I did it because I love you more than the words or diaries or even the cumulative musings of a sentimental father can ever begin to say.

'I'll write again tomorrow.

'All my love, Dad.'

I put the question to her the next morning. Should I stop writing in her diary? Could I? She screwed up her nose, the way she always had.

'You like it, don't you?' she asked.

I nodded.

'Then why stop?'

'Well, I don't know, I mean, maybe it's time for you to make your own memories.'

'*My* memories?'

I didn't understand.

'These letters aren't about me, Dad. They never were. They were always about you.'

London 2007

The boy and I went to Southgate by motorbike, old hands at this game, and – old hands again – arrived about an hour after play had started. We were dressed warmly against the autumnal chill. Middlesex had won the toss the day before and chosen to bat. Whether it was the end-of-season pitch, or indifferent form, or intemperate batting, I do not know. It may even have been brilliant bowling. Of the Middlesex batsmen, only Ed Joyce got in and he had been dismissed, caught behind off Jerome Taylor for 74. Middlesex were all out for 176 and at close of play Leicestershire were looking dangerous on 124 for one.

We find some chairs beneath the oaks at the southern end of the ground and settle in to watch. I have my usual kit –

binoculars, umbrella and a few broadsheets – but the sun is shining and it doesn't seem like a day to do crosswords. And the boy has commandeered the binoculars. While he concentrates on the cricket I watch the crowd. The people you'll find at an end-of-season, mid-table, meaningless Division 2 match are pretty much the same people you'll find at Lord's for the first match of the season. Well wrapped, well fed and well oiled. People with time on their hands. A couple of middle-aged women are knitting. A man reads the *Telegraph*. There have been rumours of rain but for the moment the sky is flecked with only a few fluffy clouds. There is the smell of things barbecuing and the sound of not very much at all. Where Lord's has its murmur, Southgate merely sighs. The ground is named for a family from the area, many of whose sons played first-class cricket and were stalwarts of the early years of Middlesex County Cricket Club. Test cricket did not start until 1877, prior to which teams would be labelled 'England' or 'an England XI', and four of the brothers played in such teams. One of them, Vyell Edward Walker, became president of the MCC in 1891. For all that it is in one of the world's great conurbations, the Walker Ground retains a curiously Victorian feel. Perhaps it is the nearby steeple of Christ Church, or perhaps it is the age of the oaks whose branches hang heavily along the southern boundary of the field. Or perhaps it is just the cricket, the cricket we play today, has survived the many depredations of the money men and television and remains, at heart, a Victorian enterprise.

Not that we much care. We're not there to see someone win or lose. We're only there for… well, for something.

We listen to conversations. A man in a leather jacket cracks open a midday beer.

'Really? She said that?' he says.

'Oh, she did. That's what she said.'

'That's all she wants? The dog?'

'Uh-huh.'

'Man, you got off easy. Gimme five.'

There is an awkward pause. The 'five' is not forthcoming on account of the second guy reaching into a bag for an M&S chilli-chicken burrito. The boy and I exchange glances.

'But I don't want her to leave,' says burrito man. He drinks deeply and takes a bite so big he gets half a mouthful of plastic wrapper. 'I got used to having her around.' Except he's speaking with his mouth full. 'Aaah dod uzd do...'

The boy is avoiding my eyes. He sits forward with his elbows on his knees. His hair covers his face. There is no way to tell what he is thinking.

That conversation again:

'It's been what? Three months?'

'Four.'

'Man.'

Pause.

'You want something else to eat? They got this new Mexican shit...'

On the other side two men are easing their way into retirement.

'I gotta talk to my accountant guy,' says one. 'Just to make sure the numbers stack up.'

'But you're not going in anyway?'

'To the office? Not much. Danny's pretty much taking care of things.'

'You've been doing it, what? Thirty years?'

'Nearer fifty,' says the first man. 'I'm seventy next month.'

'A good time to stop.'

'You're what? Sixty-nine?'

'Sixty-eight.'

'Still life in you yet.'

'Christ, "still life" is the word!'

The boy and I stand to stretch. We take a wander round the perimeter of the field. It's the lunch break and people are drinking, eating, chatting. A couple of men even have their shirts off, but none of us are fooled. Everyone else has a jumper or a coat. It's warm – but not that warm. We stop and eat a sandwich on a bench.

'Is it always like this?' he asks.

Pretty much. Except it's not always this busy.

'Sure,' I say.

'It's real quiet.'

'Yes.'

'Peaceful.'

'Yes.'

'Like the rest of the world doesn't matter.'

Yes!

After lunch the wickets start to fall. It's the Sri Lankan, Murali Kartik, playing in his first season for Middlesex, who does the damage. Ackerman falls to bring the score to 144-2. Maunders goes soon afterwards and suddenly the familiar old smell of 'collapse' is in the air. You can sense it in the crowd and on the field. Balls that would otherwise have been routine now seem like potential wicket takers as the batsmen tense up. The score becomes144 for three, then 147 for four. By the time Kartik is done, Leicestershire have lost seven wickets for seventeen runs. And they're eventually all out for 190. Question is, what will Middlesex make of the opportunity? Can they conjure a victory from this? At one point the ball is edged through the slips for four. It comes fast down to the boundary and skips off the rope and over the fence into the hand of a delighted spectator. Form on these occasions is to look pleased and lob the ball back to the nearest fielder. But there is no one fielding at fine leg or third man and the slips don't look like they can be bothered with a weary trudge to the boundary. So it falls to the spectator to throw the ball back to the fielders.

Except he doesn't. He's looking at the ball with the kind of glee and fear that kids have for properly scary movies. He's about 50. Portly without being fat, with neatly trimmed hair and a well-cut suit. He's sitting in a chair slightly apart from anyone else. Just enjoying a day's cricket on his own.

And holding the ball.

'Go on!' someone yells.

'Throw it back!'

But he doesn't move. He's standing there with everyone – not that many people but still – looking at him.

'Get on with it.'

And suddenly I realise what the problem is. *He doesn't know how to throw*. It's the most basic cricket skill, the simplest thing you learn. Before batting, before bowling, before fielding or catching or anything else, kids learn how to throw. Babies do it in their parents' living rooms or in the back garden. They stand and pick something up. And throw it. I've seen it with my own son with each passing year. I hold out my hand to the man and he gratefully passes me the ball. By this time, one of the slips – I think it was Strauss – has come most of the way to the boundary to collect the ball. I hand it to the boy wonder. A slow grin comes over his face. Half a question. I nod. And he bypasses the approaching fielder and throws the ball, low, hard and flat, to the wicket keeper.

'Good arm,' says someone behind us.

The boy smiles, but as always it's partly to himself.

'Who does he play for?' says someone else.

'He doesn't play,' I say. 'Hates the game.'

The boy doesn't bother to protest. He's done that thing he does, where he withdraws into himself. Assailed by the more mundane comments of his peers.

We don't stay the whole day. Leicestershire are all out for 190. Strauss and Godleman open the second innings for Middlesex. I haven't seen Godleman before, but he's looking nice. He and Strauss both seem to be seeing the ball okay and the pitch doesn't look dangerous. The batsmen are playing sensibly. It looks like being a draw and when Strauss falls LBW to Henderson, we decide to call it a day.

It's probably my last live match for the season. The internationals are finished. At the club there will be a couple of end-of-season friendlies, but I'm not sure I'll play. Or even get selected. It hasn't been a vintage year, for me or for England. Our club has a wonderful website. Every triumph and every failure is recorded for posterity. So I can tell you about my 2007 season. I averaged nineteen. Top score 49. Lowest score one. No ducks and no not outs. I scored 10.16 per cent of my team's runs. Not bad, but not great. And probably as good as it gets. There is nothing to suggest that I will be any better next year. The internationals might be. New Zealand first and then South Africa. That should be fun at Lord's. Always a bit of edge to those matches. Especially now that Pietersen's in the team. And Strauss, come to that, who was also born in South Africa. Matt Prior if he makes it back into the team at the expense of Ambrose. All of them continuing the great tradition of Lamb, Smith, Greig, D'Oliveira... All of them fluid in their allegiances. All of them seeking the greater stage. But especially Pietersen. He's only played South Africa in one-day matches and Twenty20. This will be his first Test series against them. The Lord's Test against South Africa is some time in July. Perfect. I must remember to apply for tickets.

'So you want to go to Lord's next year?' I ask when we're back home. 'South Africa. It'll be better than this year. Better cricket. Maybe Flintoff will be back to his best.'

'I don't know. Maybe. I don't think...' I'm not really listening. I'm busy with another flashback to the South African tour of 2003. Graeme Smith was just starting off as South African captain. A big bruiser of a man. A hard man to play and a man who plays hard. And a man in form. In the drawn first Test at Edgbaston he made a double century. At Lord's he made another as South Africa posted a mammoth 682 for six declared. England, who had been bowled out first time round for 173, were chasing the impossible total of 509. But they gave it a go – and in particular Freddie Flintoff gave it a go. He came in with the total on 208 for five and, freed from any realistic expectation of victory, proceeded to hit the South African attack all over the ground. And broke a few bats in the process. My son and I were there on the fourth day when he went on this rampage. He scored his 142 off as many balls and hit eighteen fours and five sixes. Eventually he was out trying to hit Adams to somewhere near Taunton. He missed, Boucher took off his bails and England were all out for 417. Beaten by an innings and 92 runs.

Except that the England fightback in general, and Flintoff's innings in particular, contained the impetus for an England revival. In the first two matches of that series, South Africa scored 1,410 runs for the loss of fifteen wickets. Ninety-four runs per wicket. In the next three they were bowled out in every innings at an average of 31 per wicket. The series came down to the wire at the Oval. South Africa had won at Lord's and Headingley. England won at Trent Bridge. At the Oval, South Africa made 484 in the first innings. England's reply was magnificent: 219 to Trescothick (an anagram, by the way, of 'cricket shot') and 124 to Thorpe. Vaughan, chasing victory to square the series, needed quick runs. Flintoff obliged with a rapid 95 off 104 balls and Vaughan declared on 604 for nine. Now the question was, could England bowl the visitors out a second time? Answer, an emphatic yes. I bunked off work to go to the Oval to see England win by nine wickets. Series drawn.

Eighteen months later, England won the return series in South Africa 2-1.

'So it's nicely poised,' I say. 'South Africa fancy their chances, but England should win.'[4]

'I thought it isn't about the winning?'

He's right. It isn't. Except against South Africa. An exception to the rule.

'What I mean is, it should be fun. So you'll come?'

He's stuffing his bag, a scruffy death's head rucksack. He seems to be more meticulous about his packing than usual. A pair of trainers that have been there for months go into his bag. Also a T-shirt that my son commandeered in France. A couple of books. A DVD.

'She should be home soon.'

No answer. Which is odd.

'Thanks for everything,' he says.

'A pleasure.'

Pause.

'See you soon.'

[4] Famous last words. For the first three days at Lord's, England were dominant. But then South Africa took control and won the series 2-1

'Yeah, maybe. I mean, I don't know.'

'Oh?'

He shrugs. 'Sorry.'

My mental cogs tick over slowly, but even I realise what he's saying.

'Really?'

He shrugs.

'I get to keep the dog.' He waves a stuffed toy she gave him some months before. 'Joke.'

'Oh, okay, well...'

'Yeah.'

'Listen, if I get tickets for Lord's...'

But he's already closing the door.

The house is strangely silent. Any minute now I know the kids will come in from school. There'll be the usual scramble for snacks and tea, the usual squabbles over who has whose iPod. The usual battle for the television remote. The usual chaos of bags and books, or sweaty PE kits and half-finished homework. I sit at the kitchen table and read the cricket stories. I'm feeling a little empty, a little deflated. Radio 5 tells me that Middlesex are making a fist of the match against Leicestershire. They might even be in a position to force a result.

Who cares? Not me. Not then.

Our elder daughter is first in the door.

'Hey, Dad.'

'Hello.'

'How was your day?'

'Good, fine. You?'

'Yeah, good. We dissected a frog.'

She tells me about frogs and their constituent parts. I feign interest. It's only later that we get to the elephant in the room.

'How was…?'

'*Ja*, no, he was fine. I mean, we went to the cricket.'

'Really?'

'Sure.'

'Just the two of you?'

'Uh-huh.'

She seems amused in a sad kind of way.

'So that's it?' I ask.

She hesitates and then nods. 'Did he say anything?'

'Not really. I mean, we talked about cricket.'

'Who was winning?'

I fall for it. I can't help myself.

'Cricket's not like that,' I say. 'You can't ever say who's winning. That's not what it's about.'

She's smiling at me, that old 'gotcha' smile. Those same happy-sad, thoughtful eyes.

'I know, Dad' she says. 'It never is. You taught me that, remember.'

ACKNOWLEDGEMENTS

My thanks to my editor, Andrew Goodfellow, for his patience, wisdom and insight. My thanks also to my wonderful agent, Isobel Dixon, for reading many versions and believing every one of them. I am particularly grateful to the finest group of men in England who, by happy coincidence, all play for the same cricket club in north London. I am indebted to my family. But mostly I am grateful to two young people who shall, by all that is holy, remain nameless.

Sandy Balfour plays and watches a lot of cricket. In his spare time he is a journalist, author and social activist. He is chair of the UK's leading Fairtrade chocolate company and has written four previous books including the critically acclaimed *Vulnerable in Hearts* and *Pretty Girl in Crimson Rose (8)*. He lives in London with his girlfriend and their three children.